HERSHEY'S® Kidsnacks

CHILDRENS PRESS, CHICAGO
School & Library Edition

Contents

0-516-09231-6
HERSHEY'S is a registered trademark of Hershey
Foods Corporation, Ideals Publishing Corporation, Licensee.

Copyright © MXMLXXXIV by
Hershey Foods Corporation.
All rights reserved.
Printed and bound in the
United States of America.

Published by Ideals Publishing Corporation.
11315 Watertown Plank Road
Milwaukee, WI 53226
Published simultaneously in Canada.

**All recipes developed and
tested in the HERSHEY
Test Kitchens.**

Director of Publishing Patricia Pingry
Managing Editor Marybeth Owens
Manuscript Editor Naomi Galbreath
Art Director William Scholz
Artists Cindy Hepp, Patrick McCrae
Photographer Gerald Koser
Food Stylist Carole Janis
Editorial Assistant Linda Robinson
Typography Kim Kaczanowski

Chunky Chocolate Cookies, 33
REESE'S PIECES Sugar Cookies, 31

HERSHEY'S BAKING BASICS

The recipes in this book are easy, educational, and fun for children and teens to make. Symbols next to each recipe title indicate ease of preparation. Safety factors such as handling of hot liquids and sharp instruments are also considered in these ratings...

E = easiest

M = moderately easy/difficult

D = most difficult

...Use these ratings as a general guide and remember that you are the best judge of your child's capabilities.

GENERAL TIPS

- Read the recipes carefully from beginning to end before starting any preparation.
- Measure out all ingredients before any mixing.
- Scrape down bowls often during mixing.
- Clean hands before cooking or baking.
- Wear an apron.
- Clean up as you go as well as when you are finished.

SAFETY KNOW-HOW

Remember the following tips when you are cooking or baking!

- Never work in the kitchen unless you have Mom and Dad's approval and they are close by.
- Ask Mom or Dad to help when using sharp knives and electrical appliances such as a mixer, blender, can opener, microwave oven, etc.
- Make sure floors and counters are kept free of spills, as these could cause slipping.
- Always disconnect appliances by their plugs, not their cords.
- Be sure your hands are dry when working with electrical appliances. Otherwise, you could get shocked.
- Ask Mom or Dad to remove boiling liquids from the stove top for you. Watch out for steam, too, as this can cause burns.
- Don't let pot handles hang over the stove's edge, as they could catch and tip over.
- Always use pot holders for removing hot pots or pans from stove top or oven. Be sure they are well padded and dry to prevent burns and shocks.
- When cutting and chopping, hold sharp blades away from you and your hands. Mom and Dad should always help or even complete this job for you.
- Never scrape down a mixer bowl when the mixer is running. Turn it off first, then scrape down.
- Be sure appliances are off and unplugged when changing attachments.

COOKING AND BAKING DEFINITIONS

1. Batter A thin mixture of flour and liquid which is usually combined with other ingredients to make baked products such as cakes.

2. Beat To make a mixture smooth by using a spoon in brisk, regular motion that lifts the mixture over and over, or with a rotary motion as with beater or electric mixer.

3. Blend To mix thoroughly two or more ingredients.

4. Boil To cook in water or a liquid in which bubbles rise and break on the surface. The boiling temperature of water at sea level is 212° Farenheit or 100° Centigrade.

5. Cake Pan Utensil for baking cake. It may be round, square, or oblong. Some have removable bottoms and some a tube in the center.

6. Combine To stir together two or more ingredients in a bowl.

7. Cookie Sheet A flat, rectangular utensil for baking cookies and biscuits.

8. Cream To make smooth, light and fluffy by beating with a spoon or mixer.

9. Dough A thick mixture of flour and liquid, usually combined with other ingredients to make baked products such as cookies.

10. Dry Measuring Cup Measuring cup in 1-cup, ½-cup, ⅓-cup, or ¼-cup sizes used to measure dry ingredients.

11. Fold To combine by moving a rubber spatula through two mixtures in a cutting and sliding motion.

12. Gradually Add Adding liquid or dry ingredients in small amounts to blend and prevent lumping.

13. Leavening Agent A gas-producing substance added to batter or dough to make it rise and increase in size. (In Hershey's recipes, these agents are often baking powder and baking soda.)

14. Liquid Measuring Cup Standard cup designed to measure liquid ingredients. A standard cup equals 8 fluid ounces. The standard cup for measuring liquid is usually a 1- or 2-cup size with ¼-, ⅓-, ½-, ⅔-, and ¾-cup divisions marked on the side.

15. Measuring Spoons A group of individual spoons in the following measures: 1 tablespoon, 1 teaspoon, ½ teaspoon, ¼ teaspoon. These spoons can be used to measure dry or liquid ingredients.

16. Stir To mix food materials with a spoon in a circular motion.

17. Whip To beat rapidly to add air and increase the size of ingredients such as heavy cream and egg whites.

MEASURING TIPS

- Measure ingredients such as baking powder, baking soda and salt in standard measuring spoons. Level with straight-edged spatula or knife. Do not use kitchen flatware as measuring equipment.
- Measure butter or margarine by using indicators on wrapper.
- Measure solid shortening in standard measuring cups by packing with a spatula to eliminate air pockets. Level with a straight-edged spatula or knife.
- Measure flour and other dry ingredients by lightly spooning into nested measuring cups. Level with a straight-edged spatula or knife.
- Measure liquids in a regular liquid measuring cup; read amounts at eye level.
- Measure brown sugar by packing firmly into a nested measuring cup with back of spoon; sugar should hold its shape when turned out of cup.
- Do not measure ingredients directly over your mixing bowl. This could cause wasted ingredients or failures.

BAKING TIPS

- Preheat oven for five minutes before baking.
- Ingredients should be at room temperature for the best baking results.
- Use standard size pans called for in the recipes. We use shiny metal pans. If using heat-proof glass pans, reduce oven temperature by 25° F.
- Check for expiration dates on baking powder and baking soda. Aged leavening agents will cause baked goods to rise improperly.
- Check oven temperature periodically with an accurate oven thermometer.
- Be sure baking pans or cookie sheets are placed in the center of the oven; for best results, bake on only one rack.
- Allow spaces in oven between baking pans or sheets while baking. At least two inches of space are needed around the sides of the oven for proper heat circulation.
- Do not use sheets of aluminum foil on oven racks or on bottom of oven. This can cause failures.

MEASURING EQUIVALENTS

3 teaspoons = 1 tablespoon

½ tablespoon = 1½ teaspoons

4 tablespoons = ¼ cup

5 tablespoons plus 1 teaspoon = ⅓ cup

16 tablespoons = 1 cup

2 cups = 1 pint

4 cups (or 2 pints) = 1 quart

4 quarts = 1 gallon

HINTS ON WHIPPING CREAM

- Cream whips best when cream, bowl and beaters are well chilled.
- Use heavy (whipping) cream to make whipped cream; it contains 36% to 40% milk fat.
- Whipped cream has a foam that is thick, smooth and glossy. The cream should increase two times in size when whipped.
- Do not overbeat or cream will separate and develop lumps.

BAKEWARE

  Square Pan

 Pie Pan

 13" x 9" Oblong Pan

 Round Cake Pan

 Custard Cup

 Tube Pan

 Muffin Tin

 Cookie Sheet

 9" x 5" Loaf Pan

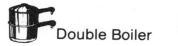 Jelly Roll Pan

 Wire Cooling Rack

COOKWARE AND SMALL UTENSILS

 Saucepan

 Double Boiler

 Mixing Bowls

 Rolling Pin

 Cutting Board

 Rotary Beater

 Liquid Measuring Cup

 Dry Measuring Cups

OTHER SMALL UTENSILS

 Wire Whisk

 Wooden Spoon

 Metal Spatula

 Rubber Spatula

 Pie Server

 Paring Knife

 Cookie Spatula

 Kitchen Shears

 Juicer

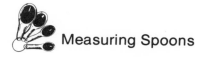 Cookie Cutters

Ice Cream Scoop

Parer

Pastry Blender

Measuring Spoons

CHOCOLATE AND COCOA DEFINITIONS

ARTIFICIAL CHOCOLATE — an imitation product that does not contain ingredients made from cocoa beans. Sometimes imitation products do not contain milk or sugar either. (Hershey does not make artificial chocolate.)

BITTER CHOCOLATE — chocolate liquor which has been cooled and usually made into blocks. Bitter chocolate is sometimes called unsweetened chocolate or baking chocolate.

CHOCOLATE — unsweetened chocolate or chocolate liquor.

CHOCOLATE FLAVORED — used to describe food products flavored with cocoa and/or chocolate liquor, but which do not contain enough of these products to be called chocolate.

CHOCOLATE FLAVORED SYRUP — a combination of chocolate liquor or cocoa, sugar, water, salt and sometimes other flavorings such as vanilla.

CHOCOLATE LIQUOR — the basic material of all chocolate products. It is the liquid made from the "meat" of the cocoa bean (called the nib). Chocolate liquor has no alcoholic content.

COCOA — an all-natural powdered chocolate product made from roasted cocoa beans with most of the fat (known as cocoa butter) removed. Cocoa provides a concentrated flavor for making chocolate desserts. (Hershey's Cocoa is pure because it contains no additives or preservatives.)

COCOA BEANS — the fruit of the cacao tree which grows mainly in West Africa, Latin and South America, Indonesia, and other Pacific basin countries. Cocoa and chocolate are made from cocoa beans.

COCOA BUTTER — a vegetable fat in chocolate liquor.

MILK CHOCOLATE — a combination of chocolate liquor, added cocoa butter, sugar and milk or cream. It must contain at least 10% chocolate liquor.

SEMI-SWEET CHOCOLATE — a combination of chocolate liquor, added cocoa butter and sugar which must contain at least 35% chocolate liquor.

SWEET CHOCOLATE — a combination of chocolate liquor, added cocoa butter and sugar which must contain at least 15% chocolate liquor. Sweet chocolate has a higher proportion of sugar than semi-sweet chocolate.

SOME FACTS ABOUT CHOCOLATE

Real chocolate contains a vegetable fat called cocoa butter. Because chocolate contains cocoa butter, it is sensitive to heat and humidity.

Temperatures of 78° Farenheit or more cause chocolate to melt and the cocoa butter in it to rise to the surface. If this happens, you will see a gray appearance on the surface of the chocolate known as cocoa butter "bloom."

Sugar bloom may also occur on the surface of sweet, semi-sweet, or milk chocolate on humid days. Droplets of moisture on chocolate caused by humidity make the sugar in the chocolate dissolve and rise to the surface, causing a gray appearance. Chocolate can be refrigerated on hot, humid days, but may "bloom" when brought to room temperature.

The quality and flavor of chocolate is not affected by cocoa butter bloom or sugar bloom. The gray appearance will disappear when the chocolate is melted. To avoid bloom, store chocolate in a cool, dry place. The best storage temperature is between 65° and 70° Farenheit. Chocolate products generally stay fresh over one year when stored properly.

When melting chocolate, break into 1-inch pieces and melt in the top of a double boiler over hot (*but not boiling*) water. *Never* let the water boil. Chocolate that is melted over too high heat will become grainy and thick. Watch heat carefully because chocolate scorches easily!

Never add water to melted chocolate to make thinner. This will not work and will cause the product to become grainy and thick. Be sure cooking utensils and pans are free of all water, too, because even a drop can ruin melted chocolate.

INFORMATION ABOUT REESE'S PEANUT BUTTER FLAVORED CHIPS

Reese's Peanut Butter Flavored Chips are made from real peanuts and contain no preservatives or artificial peanut flavoring. They are called "flavored" because they are made with peanut meal instead of peanut butter. Reese's Peanut Butter Chips contain some protein, riboflavin, niacin, calcium, and iron. They can be used whole or melted and combined with other ingredients to make peanut butter flavored desserts.

Like chocolate, peanut butter chips will scorch and become too thick when melted over too high heat. Melt in the top of a double boiler over hot (but *not* boiling) water. And, never add water to melted peanut butter chips to make thinner. This will not work and will cause the product to become even thicker. Be sure cooking utensils and pans are free from water too.

Chips, Chips and More

D CHOCOLATE CHIP ANGEL CAKE

Yield: about 12 servings

18-ounce package "two-step" angel food cake mix
1 cup HERSHEY'S MINI CHIPS
Milk Chocolate Frosting (recipe follows)

1. Prepare cake batter according to package directions.*
2. Fold in HERSHEY'S MINI CHIPS.
3. Pour batter into an *un*greased 10-inch tube pan.
4. Cut through batter with dull knife or spatula to remove air bubbles.
5. Bake at 375° for 30 to 40 minutes or until golden brown. (Do not underbake.)
6. Turn pan upside down on funnel or bottle to cool.
7. Cool completely in pan.
8. Carefully run a knife along side of pan to loosen cake.
9. Place on serving plate and frost with Milk Chocolate Frosting.

*See this page for Tips on Preparing Angel Food Cakes.

Milk Chocolate Frosting

11.5-ounce package (2 cups) HERSHEY'S Milk Chocolate Chips
8-ounce container (3½ cups) frozen non-dairy whipped topping, thawed

1. Melt HERSHEY'S Milk Chocolate Chips in top of double boiler over hot (*not* boiling) water, stirring constantly.
2. Fold into whipped topping until blended and spreadable.
3. Use immediately.

Tips on Preparing Angel Food Cakes

- Be sure mixing bowl, beaters, spatula and measuring cups are very clean and free of grease. (Even the slightest bit of grease can prevent angel food batter from whipping properly.)
- Do not use a plastic bowl for mixing, as this too can prevent proper whipping.
- Beat at highest speed until egg whites are *very* stiff. Check by cutting a "trench" through beaten egg whites with spatula. If trench does not hold shape, beat longer. (Beating should take 5 to 10 minutes, depending on mixer used.)
- Bake on lowest rack, removing top rack *before* preheating oven.
- Do *not* underbake, as this will cause cake to fall from pan when inverted. Top crust should look golden brown and feel firm and dry.
- Hanging pan upside down to cool allows cake to set without collapsing.

Chocolate Chip Angel Cake

E DOTTED SWISS

Yield: about 12 ounces candy

**12-ounce package (2 cups) HERSHEY'S
Semi-Sweet Chocolate chips
Colored decorator cake sprinkles**

1. Line a cookie sheet with wax paper; set aside.
2. Melt HERSHEY'S Semi-Sweet Chocolate Chips in top of double boiler over hot (*not* boiling) water.
3. Spread chocolate to desired thickness on wax paper-lined cookie sheet.
4. Immediately shake sprinkles evenly onto chocolate, as desired.
5. Let stand at room temperature until chocolate is set.
6. Cut or break to serve.

E PEANUTTY SNACK CAKE

Yield: about 8 servings

**13.5-ounce package banana walnut snack
cake mix
1 cup REESE'S Peanut Butter Chips**

1. Prepare cake batter in an 8-inch square pan according to package directions.
2. Sprinkle REESE'S Peanut Butter Chips evenly over batter in pan.
3. Bake according to package directions.
4. Serve warm or cool.

D CHOCO-CHIP UPSIDE DOWN CAKE

Yield: about 9 servings

**¾ cup apple jelly
16-ounce package pound cake mix
5.75-ounce package (1 cup) HERSHEY'S Milk
Chocolate Chips**

1. Grease and flour a 9-inch square pan.
2. Spread jelly evenly onto bottom of prepared pan; set aside.
3. Prepare cake batter according to package directions.
4. Stir in ½ cup of the HERSHEY'S Milk Chocolate Chips.
5. Pour batter over jelly in pan, spreading gently and evenly.
6. Sprinkle with remaining ½ cup milk chocolate chips.
7. Bake at 325° for 50 to 55 minutes or until cake springs back when touched lightly.
8. Cool 5 minutes in pan.
9. Invert onto serving plate.
10. Cool about 10 minutes.
11. Serve warm.

M MINI CHIP PANCAKE CRITTERS

Yield: about 14 pancakes

**16-ounce carton frozen pancake batter,
thawed
½ cup HERSHEY'S MINI CHIPS
Butter and pancake syrup**

1. Pour pancake batter into a small bowl.
2. Stir in HERSHEY'S MINI CHIPS.
3. Prepare pancakes according to package directions, dropping batter into desired animal shapes.
4. Serve warm with butter and pancake syrup.

FUDGEY PEANUT BUTTER CAKE

Yield: about 12 servings

3.5-ounce package instant vanilla pudding and pie filling mix
1¼ cups cold milk
1 cup REESE'S Peanut Butter Chips
18.25 or 18.5-ounce package yellow cake mix
16-ounce can (1½ cups) HERSHEY'S Chocolate Fudge Topping

1. Combine pudding mix with *1 cup* of the milk in a small mixer bowl.
2. Beat on low speed 2 minutes; set aside.
3. Melt REESE'S Peanut Butter Chips with remaining ¼ cup milk in top of double boiler over hot (*not* boiling) water, stirring constantly until blended.
4. Gradually add peanut butter mixture *while warm* to pudding, beating well on low speed after each addition.
5. Beat on medium to high speed an additional 1 minute.
6. Cover and refrigerate at least 2 hours or until spreadable.
7. Meanwhile, prepare cake batter according to package directions for 8- or 9-inch round layers; cool completely.
8. Fill and frost cake layers with chilled peanut butter pudding mixture.
9. Cover and chill overnight.
10. Heat HERSHEY'S Chocolate Fudge Topping *just* to lukewarm according to label directions.
11. Carefully spoon and spread half of fudge topping (about ¾ cup) over chilled cake, allowing it to drizzle down sides.
12. Serve immediately with remaining fudge topping; refrigerate leftovers.

PEANUTTY TORTONI

Yield: about 12 servings

1 cup REESE'S Peanut Butter Chips
2 cups heavy (whipping) cream
1 cup coconut cookie crumbs*
½ cup unsifted confectioners' sugar
2 teaspoons vanilla
Drained maraschino cherry halves

1. Place paper liners in 2½-inch muffin cups; set aside.
2. Chop REESE'S Peanut Butter Chips in nut chopper or by hand. (Do *not* use blender or food processor.) Set aside.
3. Combine *1 cup* of the (*un*whipped) heavy cream with the coconut cookie crumbs, confectioners' sugar and vanilla.
4. Cover and chill 30 minutes.
5. Beat remaining 1 cup heavy cream on high speed until stiff.
6. Fold in chilled cream-cookie crumb mixture and chopped peanut butter chips.
7. Fill paper-lined muffin cups full with mixture.
8. Cover and freeze overnight.
9. Top with maraschino cherry halves just before serving.

*Any type hard coconut cookie may be used. Use blender or food processor to make crumbs.

M NEOPOLITAN POUND CAKE

Yield: about 8 servings

16-ounce package pound cake mix
¼ cup HERSHEY'S Syrup
¼ cup HERSHEY'S MINI CHIPS
¼ teaspoon unsweetened strawberry
flavored drink mix
Ice cream and additional HERSHEY'S
Syrup

1. Grease a 9 x 5-inch loaf pan and line bottom with wax paper; set aside.
2. Prepare cake batter according to package directions.
3. Divide into 3 portions, about 1⅓ cups each.
4. Stir HERSHEY'S Syrup and MINI CHIPS into one portion; set aside.
5. Stir strawberry flavored drink mix into second portion.
6. Pour strawberry batter into prepared pan.
7. Gently spoon and spread plain batter onto strawberry batter in pan.
8. Top with chocolate batter.
9. Bake at 325° for 60 to 70 minutes or until cake tester inserted comes out clean.
10. Cool 10 to 15 minutes in pan.
11. Carefully run a knife along sides of pan to loosen cake.
12. Remove cake from pan onto wire rack to cool completely.
13. Serve with ice cream and additional HERSHEY'S Syrup.

Prepare pan and cake batters.

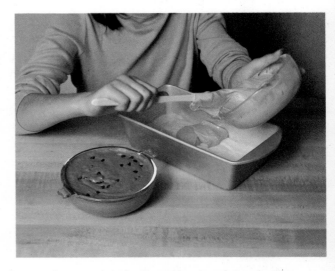

Spoon plain batter onto strawberry batter.

Spoon chocolate batter onto plain batter.

Neopolitan Pound Cake, this page

PEANUT BUTTER MARBLE CAKE

Yield: about 12 servings

> **18.25 or 18.5-ounce package white cake mix**
> **1 cup REESE'S Peanut Butter Chips**
> **⅓ cup milk**
> **16-ounce can any flavor ready-to-spread frosting**

1. Grease two 8- or 9-inch round cake pans and line bottoms with wax paper; set aside.
2. Prepare cake batter according to package directions.
3. Measure out 1 cup of the batter; set aside.
4. Pour remaining batter into prepared cake pans; set aside.
5. Melt REESE'S Peanut Butter Chips with milk in top of double boiler over hot (*not* boiling) water, stirring constantly until blended.
6. Stir melted peanut butter mixture *while warm* into reserved 1 cup batter until blended.
7. Place heaping tablespoonfuls of peanut butter batter on top of batter in pans.
8. Use a knife or spatula to lift and swirl batter for a marbled appearance.
9. Bake at 350° for 30 to 35 minutes or until cake begins to pull away from sides of pans.
10. Cool 10 to 15 minutes in pans.
11. Carefully run a knife along sides of pans to loosen cake.
12. Remove cake from pans onto wire rack to cool completely.
13. Fill and frost with ready-to-spread frosting.

 ## EASY MINI CHIP COFFEECAKE

Yield: about 6 servings

> **10.5-ounce package "easy mix" coffeecake**
> **¾ cup HERSHEY'S MINI CHIPS**

1. Prepare coffeecake batter according to package directions.
2. Stir in ½ *cup* of the HERSHEY'S MINI CHIPS.
3. Pour into pan as directed on package.
4. Sprinkle with topping from package and remaining ¼ cup MINI CHIPS.
5. Bake at 375° for 30 minutes.
6. Serve warm.

 ## PEANUT BUTTER CHIP FRUITCAKE

Yield: about 8 servings

> **17-ounce package date quick bread mix**
> **¼ cup water**
> **1 egg**
> **¾ cup mincemeat**
> **1 cup mixed candied fruit**
> **1 cup chopped nuts**
> **1 cup REESE'S Peanut Butter Chips**

1. Grease a 9 x 5-inch loaf pan and line bottom with wax paper; set aside.
2. Thoroughly combine all ingredients with spoon in large mixing bowl.
3. Pour batter into prepared pan.
4. Bake at 350° for 60 to 65 minutes or until a toothpick inserted comes out clean.
5. Cool 15 minutes in pan.
6. Carefully run a knife along sides of pan to loosen cake.
7. Remove cake from pan onto wire rack to cool completely.
8. Wrap tightly in foil or plastic wrap.
9. Store overnight before serving.

Ⓓ PEANUT BUTTER 'N ICE CREAM CAKE

Yield: about 12 servings

18.25 or 18.5-ounce package yellow cake mix
1½ cups REESE'S Peanut Butter Chips
½ cup milk
½ gallon vanilla or chocolate ice cream, softened
2 16-ounce containers any flavor ready-to-spread frosting

1. Grease two 9-inch round cake pans and line bottoms with wax paper; set aside.
2. Prepare cake batter according to package directions; set aside.
3. Melt REESE'S Peanut Butter Chips with milk in top of double boiler over hot (*not* boiling) water, stirring constantly until blended.
4. Add peanut butter mixture *while warm* to cake batter.
5. Beat on medium speed until blended, about 2 minutes.
6. Pour batter into prepared pans.
7. Bake at 350° for 30 to 35 minutes or until cake begins to pull away from sides of pans.
8. Cool 10 to 15 minutes in pans.
9. Carefully run knife along sides of pans to loosen cake.
10. Remove cake from pans onto wire rack to cool completely.
11. Meanwhile, line bottom and sides of three 9-inch round cake pans with aluminum foil.
12. Let ice cream stand at room temperature a few minutes to soften.
13. Divide and spread evenly among prepared pans.
14. Cover and freeze overnight.
15. Carefully cut cooled cake layers in half horizontally to make 4 thin layers.
16. Remove ice cream layers from freezer, *one at a time,* as needed for next steps.
17. Alternately stack cake and ice cream layers, beginning and ending with cake.
18. Cover and freeze overnight.
19. Working quickly, frost cake with one container ready-to-spread frosting.
20. Return to freezer until frosting is firm, about 15 minutes.
21. Frost with second container of frosting.
22. Cover and freeze until ready to serve.

Ⓓ CREAMY PEANUT BUTTER PIE

Yield: about 6 servings

3-ounce package cream cheese
1 teaspoon lemon juice
1 cup REESE'S Peanut Butter Chips
⅔ cup sweetened condensed milk
½ cup heavy (whipping) cream
6-ounce packaged graham cracker pie crust
Whipped Cream Topping (recipe follows)
Additional REESE'S Peanut Butter Chips

1. Beat cream cheese and lemon juice on medium speed in small mixer bowl until fluffy, about 2 minutes; set aside.
2. Melt REESE'S Peanut Butter Chips with condensed milk in top of double boiler over hot (*not* boiling) water, stirring constantly.
3. Add peanut butter mixture *while warm* to cream cheese.
4. Beat on medium speed until blended, about 1 minute.
5. Cool 5 minutes at room temperature.
6. Whip cream until stiff.
7. Fold in peanut butter mixture.
8. Pour into crust.
9. Cover and chill overnight.
10. Spread Whipped Cream Topping over filling and sprinkle with additional peanut butter chips just before serving; refrigerate leftovers.

Whipped Cream Topping

½ cup heavy (whipping) cream
1 tablespoon unsifted confectioners' sugar
½ teaspoon vanilla

1. Combine all Topping ingredients in a small mixer bowl.
2. Whip until stiff.

CHOCO-PEANUT BUTTER DROPS

Yield: about 30 drops

6-ounce package (1 cup) HERSHEY'S Semi-Sweet Chocolate Chips
⅔ cup sweetened condensed milk
½ cup miniature marshmallows
½ cup coarsely chopped peanuts
¼ cup peanut butter
1 teaspoon vanilla

1. Melt HERSHEY'S Semi-Sweet Chocolate Chips in top of double boiler over hot (*not* boiling) water, stirring constantly.
2. Add condensed milk and marshmallows.
3. Stir constantly until marshmallows are melted and blended.
4. Remove from heat and stir in chopped peanuts, peanut butter and vanilla until peanut butter and vanilla are blended.
5. Drop by rounded teaspoonfuls into paper or foil petite four cups (miniature muffin cups).
6. Cover and chill 15 minutes before serving; refrigerate leftovers.

 ## RAINBOW SLICES

Yield: about 36 slices

12-ounce package (2 cups) HERSHEY'S Semi-Sweet Chocolate Chips
½ cup butter or margarine
10½-ounce package (6 cups) colored and flavored miniature marshmallows
1 cup finely chopped nuts
Additional chopped nuts

1. Melt HERSHEY'S Semi-Sweet Chocolate Chips with butter or margarine in medium saucepan over low to medium heat, stirring constantly until blended.
2. Remove from heat and cool at room temperature 5 minutes.
3. Stir in marshmallows and nuts. (Do *not* melt marshmallows.)
4. Shape mixture into two 1½-inch to 2-inch diameter rolls on wax paper.
5. Wrap and chill 15 minutes.
6. Roll in chopped nuts.
7. Wrap and chill overnight.
8. Slice rolls into ¼-inch slices.
9. Store in a cool, dry place.

 ## DOUBLE PEANUT CLUSTERS

Yield: about 2 dozen

12-ounce package (2 cups) REESE'S Peanut Butter Chips
1 tablespoon shortening
2 cups salted peanuts

1. Line a cookie sheet with wax paper; set aside.
2. Melt REESE'S Peanut Butter Chips with shortening in top of double boiler over hot (*not* boiling) water, stirring constantly until blended.
3. Remove from heat and stir in peanuts.
4. Drop by rounded teaspoonfuls onto wax paper-lined cookie sheet.
5. Cool until set.
6. Store in a cool, dry place.

D GEORGIA ICE CREAM

Yield: about 2 quarts

**12-ounce package (2 cups) REESE'S Peanut
  Butter Chips**
2 cups light cream
½ cup sugar
¼ teaspoon salt
21-ounce can peach pie filling
2 teaspoons vanilla
1 cup heavy (whipping) cream

1. Melt REESE'S Peanut Butter Chips with light
   cream, sugar and salt in a medium saucepan over low to medium heat, stirring constantly until blended.
2. Remove from heat and stir in peach pie filling and vanilla.
3. Cool completely at room temperature.
4. Beat heavy cream on high speed until stiff.
5. Fold into cooled peanut butter chip-peach
   mixture.
6. Pour into a 2- to 3-quart freezer-proof container.
7. Cover and freeze overnight.

E A-B-C CHOCOLATE CLUSTERS

Yield: about 18 clusters

**5.75-ounce package (1 cup) HERSHEY'S Milk
  Chocolate Chips**
**1 teaspoon shortening (*not* butter, margarine
  or oil)**
1 cup alphabet-shaped cereal
¼ cup raisins

1. Line a cookie sheet with wax paper; set
   aside.
2. Melt HERSHEY'S Milk Chocolate Chips with
   shortening in top of double boiler over hot
   (*not* boiling) water, stirring constantly until
   blended.
3. Remove from heat and stir in cereal and
   raisins.
4. Drop by rounded teaspoonfuls onto wax
   paper-lined cookie sheet.
5. Cover and chill 15 minutes before serving.
6. Store in a cool, dry place.

M PEANUT BUTTER 'N JELLY COFFEECAKE

Yield: about 8 servings

2 cups buttermilk baking mix
2 tablespoons sugar
1 egg
⅔ cup milk
2 tablespoons vegetable oil
1½ cups REESE'S Peanut Butter Chips
½ cup any flavor jelly or preserves

1. Grease a 9-inch square pan; set aside.
2. Combine buttermilk baking mix, sugar, egg,
   milk and oil in a large mixer bowl.
3. Beat on medium speed until blended and
   smooth, about 1 minute.
4. Stir in *1 cup* of the REESE'S Peanut Butter
   Chips.
5. Spread batter in prepared pan.
6. Bake at 400° for 20 to 25 minutes, or until
   cake tester inserted comes out clean.
7. Remove from oven and spread jelly or preserves evenly on top.
8. Sprinkle with remaining ½ cup peanut butter chips.
9. Let stand 15 minutes before serving.
10. Serve warm.

SUPER QUICK PEANUT BUTTER CHIP BREAD

Yield: about 8 servings

16.1-ounce package nut quick bread mix
1 cup REESE'S Peanut Butter Chips
Confectioners' sugar

1. Prepare quick bread batter according to package directions.

2. Stir in REESE'S Peanut Butter Chips.
3. Bake according to package directions; cool completely.
4. Sprinkle with confectioners' sugar just before serving.

 ## MINI CHIP BANANA MUFFINS

Yield: about 12 muffins

11.5-ounce package banana nut muffin mix
½ cup HERSHEY'S MINI CHIPS
Butter

1. Place paper liners in 2½-inch muffin cups; set aside.

2. Prepare muffin batter according to package directions.
3. Stir in HERSHEY'S MINI CHIPS.
4. Bake in paper-lined muffin cups according to package directions.
5. Serve warm with butter.

PEANUT BUTTER PUDDIN' CAKE

Yield: about 8 servings

13.5-ounce package applesauce raisin snack cake mix
12-ounce package (2 cups) REESE'S Peanut Butter Chips
1⅓ cups packed light brown sugar
1¼ cups water
1 tablespoon lemon juice
1 tablespoon butter or margarine
Whipped topping

1. Prepare cake batter in a 9-inch square pan according to package directions.
2. Stir in *1 cup* of the REESE'S Peanut Butter Chips.

3. Sprinkle remaining 1 cup peanut butter chips evenly over batter in pan; set aside.
4. Combine brown sugar, water, lemon juice and butter or margarine in a 2-quart saucepan.
5. Stir constantly over medium heat until mixture comes to a full boil.
6. Carefully pour hot mixture over batter in pan. (*Do not stir.*)
7. Bake at 350° for 45 minutes.
8. Let stand 15 minutes before serving.
9. Serve warm with whipped topping.

M FRUITY PEANUT BUTTER CHIP CRUMBLE

Yield: about 8 servings

> **21-ounce can apple, peach, apricot or blueberry pie filling**
> **8-ounce package (single layer) yellow cake mix**
> **1 cup REESE'S Peanut Butter Chips**
> **¼ cup butter or margarine**
> **Ice cream or whipped topping**

1. Grease an 8-inch square pan.
2. Spread pie filling in prepared pan; set aside.
3. Combine dry cake mix with *½ cup* of the REESE'S Peanut Butter Chips.
4. Sprinkle evenly over pie filling in pan. (*Do not stir.*) Set aside.
5. Melt butter or margarine in small saucepan over low heat. (Watch carefully.)
6. Drizzle evenly on cake mix in pan.
7. Bake at 375° for 40 to 45 minutes or until golden brown.
8. Immediately sprinkle with remaining ½ cup peanut butter chips.
9. Let stand 10 minutes before serving.
10. Serve warm with ice cream or whipped topping.

CRUNCHY NUTTY ICE CREAM PARFAITS

Yield: 4 to 6 parfaits

> **Peanut Butter Sauce (recipe follows)**
> **Coconut Crunch (recipe follows)**
> **1 pint vanilla ice cream**

Peanut Butter Sauce

> **1 cup REESE'S Peanut Butter Chips**
> **⅓ cup milk**
> **¼ cup heavy (whipping) cream**
> **¼ teaspoon vanilla**

1. Melt REESE'S Peanut Butter Chips with milk and heavy cream in medium saucepan, stirring constantly, over low heat until blended.
2. Remove from heat and stir in vanilla.
3. Cool to room temperature.
4. Meanwhile, prepare Coconut Crunch.

Coconut Crunch

> **¼ cup flaked coconut**
> **¼ cup chopped nuts**
> **2 teaspoons butter or margarine**

1. Place Coconut Crunch ingredients in an 8- or 9-inch square pan.
2. Toast in a 325° oven, stirring occasionally, for 6 to 8 minutes or until butter or margarine is melted and mixture is very lightly browned. (Watch carefully.)
3. Cool to room temperature.

To Make Parfaits

1. Place 1 tablespoon Peanut Butter Sauce in bottom of parfait glass.
2. Add 1 small scoop vanilla ice cream.
3. Top with 1 additional tablespoon Sauce.
4. Sprinkle with 1 tablespoon Coconut Crunch.
5. Add another scoop ice cream.
6. Top with additional Sauce and Crunch.
7. Repeat steps 1 through 6 to prepare remaining parfaits.
8. Serve immediately.

these crayons belong to

Kelly
name

Cut-outs and Critters

 EASY PEANUT BUTTER CUT-OUTS

Yield: 24 2 to 3-inch cut-outs

> **12-ounce package (2 cups) REESE'S Peanut Butter Chips**
> **14-ounce can (1⅓ cups) sweetened condensed milk**
> **Tinted vanilla ready-to-spread frosting, colored gels, candy sprinkles, raisins, etc.**

1. Line a large cookie sheet with aluminum foil.
2. Lightly butter foil; set aside.
3. Combine REESE'S Peanut Butter Chips and condensed milk in large micro-proof bowl.
4. Microwave on high (full power) for 1½ minutes or until peanut butter chips are softened.
5. Stir until chips are melted and blended. (If necessary, microwave on high a few additional seconds to melt chips.)*
6. Place mixture on foil-lined, buttered cookie sheet.
7. With clean, lightly buttered fingers, pat mixture into a 13 x 11-inch rectangle.
8. Smooth surface with a rolling pin.
9. Cool at room temperature 30 minutes.
10. Cover tightly and chill until firm, about 1 hour.
11. Cut into desired shapes with cookie cutters.
12. Paint on features, clothes, etc., with tinted frosting and decorate with gels, sprinkles, raisins, etc., as desired.

*Or, melt and blend in top of double boiler over hot water.

Easy Peanut Butter Cut-Outs

Prepare cookie sheet and ingredients.

Pat peanut butter mixture into a rectangle.

Cut into shapes and decorate as desired.

PEANUTTY ANIMAL CRACKERS

Yield: about 48 cookies

> **1 cup REESE'S Peanut Butter Chips**
> **1 tablespoon shortening (do *not* use butter, margarine or oil)**
> **2 2-ounce boxes animal crackers**
> **HERSHEY'S MINI CHIPS**

1. Melt REESE'S Peanut Butter Chips with shortening in top of double boiler over hot (*not* boiling) water, stirring constantly until blended.
2. Remove from heat but leave top of double boiler over water.
3. Use tongs or fork to carefully dip animal cracker into warm peanut butter mixture.
4. Hold dipped cracker over peanut butter mixture in pan to allow extra coating to drip off.
5. Place coated cracker on wax paper.
6. Use HERSHEY'S MINI CHIPS to form eyes, nose and mouth, as desired.
7. Repeat steps 3 through 6 until all animal crackers are coated.
8. Allow coating to harden at room temperature.
9. Store in a cool, dry place.

MINI CHIP PUZZLE COOKIES

Yield: about 48 pieces

> **15-ounce package sugar cookie mix**
> **1 cup HERSHEY'S MINI CHIPS**

1. Prepare cookie dough according to package directions.
2. Stir in HERSHEY'S MINI CHIPS.
3. Shape dough into a ball and place on an ungreased 17 x 14-inch (or larger) cookie sheet.
4. Roll dough into a 14 x 12-inch oval or rectangle on cookie sheet with floured rolling pin or flatten with clean, floured hands. (Be sure to leave at least a 2-inch border between edge of dough and cookie sheet.)
5. Bake at 375° for 10 to 12 minutes or until *very* lightly browned.
6. Immediately cut warm cookie into desired 1- to 2-inch puzzle shapes using sharp knife. (Use a pot holder to firmly grasp cookie sheet with free hand.)
7. Allow to cool completely on cookie sheet.
8. Carefully remove cooled pieces from cookie sheet with spatula and reassemble into puzzle.

[M] CUT-UP CRITTERS CAKE

18.25 or 18.5-ounce package yellow cake mix
1½ cups REESE'S Peanut Butter Chips
½ cup milk

1. Grease two 9-inch round cake pans and line bottoms with wax paper; set aside.
2. Prepare cake batter according to package directions; set aside.
3. Melt REESE'S Peanut Butter Chips with milk in top of double boiler over hot (*not* boiling) water, stirring constantly until blended.
4. Add peanut butter mixture *while warm* to cake batter.
5. Beat on medium speed until blended, about 2 minutes.
6. Pour batter into prepared pans.
7. Bake at 350° for 30 to 35 minutes or until cake begins to pull away from sides of pans.
8. Cool 10 to 15 minutes in pans.
9. Carefully run knife along sides of pans to loosen cake.
10. Remove cake from pans onto wire rack to cool completely.
11. Cut and decorate as directed to make any of the following "critters."

PEANUTTY BUNNY

Yield: about 12 servings

To form bunny:

1. Following the diagram, cut one layer of the Cut-Up Critters Cake (this page) to form bunny ears, about 6" x 1".
2. Place cut layer next to second layer to form bunny head and body.
3. Place ears as shown.

To decorate:

16-ounce container creamy vanilla ready-to-spread frosting
½ cup flaked coconut
1 marshmallow, cut in half crosswise (eyes)
2 HERSHEY'S Chocolate Chips (pupils)
1 pink square mint (nose)
2 squares candy-coated gum (teeth)
6 4-inch strands black shoestring licorice (whiskers)
1 flattened marshmallow (tail)

1. Frost with ready-to-spread frosting.
2. Sprinkle coconut over all.
3. Form eyes, nose, teeth, whiskers and tail as shown in diagram.

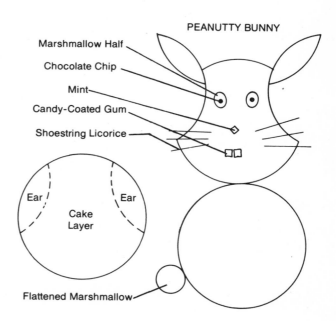

PEANUTTY BUNNY

Marshmallow Half
Chocolate Chip
Mint
Candy-Coated Gum
Shoestring Licorice

Ear Ear
Cake Layer

Flattened Marshmallow

PEANUTTY OWL

Yield: about 12 servings

To form owl:

1. Following the diagram, cut one layer of the Cut-Up Critters Cake (page 25) to form owl ears, about 2" x 1".
2. Cut second layer as shown to form owl body.
3. Place first cut layer next to second layer to form owl head and body.
4. Place ears as shown.

To decorate:

16-ounce container creamy chocolate ready-to-spread frosting
1 marshmallow, cut in half crosswise (eyes)
2 HERSHEY'S Chocolate Chips (pupils)
3-inch carrot wedge (beak)

1. Frost with ready-to-spread frosting.
2. Form eyes and beak as shown in diagram.

PEANUTTY MOUSE

Yield: about 12 servings

To form mouse:

Following the diagram, place one layer of the Cut-Up Critters Cake (page 25) next to second layer to form mouse head and body.

To decorate:

16-ounce container creamy vanilla ready-to-spread frosting
2 chocolate wafer cookies (ears)
1 marshmallow, cut in half crosswise (eyes)
2 orange REESE'S PIECES candy (pupils)
1 brown REESE'S PIECES candy (nose)
4 4-inch strands black shoestring licorice (whiskers)
3-inch strand black shoestring licorice (mouth)
6-inch strand black shoestring licorice (tail)
Decorator Frostings

1. Frost with ready-to-spread frosting.
2. Form ears, eyes, nose, mouth, whiskers and tail as shown in diagram.
3. Decorate with Decorator Frostings as desired.

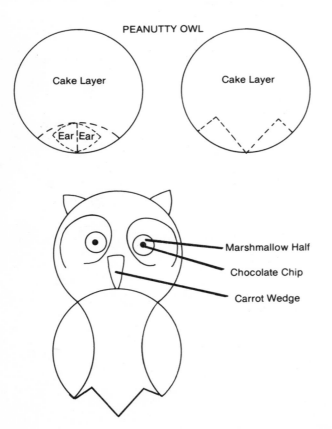

PEANUTTY OWL

Cake Layer

Cake Layer

Ear | Ear

Marshmallow Half
Chocolate Chip
Carrot Wedge

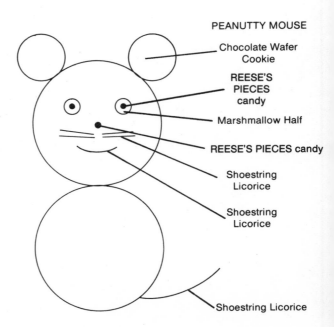

PEANUTTY MOUSE

Chocolate Wafer Cookie

REESE'S PIECES candy

Marshmallow Half

REESE'S PIECES candy

Shoestring Licorice

Shoestring Licorice

Shoestring Licorice

81092

Cookies 'n Brownies Galore

E NUTTY NO-BAKE COCOA BALLS

Yield: about 60 balls

- **3½ cups unsifted confectioners' sugar**
- **¾ cup HERSHEY'S Cocoa**
- **14-ounce can (1⅓ cups) sweetened condensed milk**
- **1 teaspoon vanilla**
- **2 cups finely chopped nuts**
- **Additional confectioners' sugar**

1. Combine confectioners' sugar and cocoa in large mixer bowl.
2. Add condensed milk and vanilla.
3. Beat on medium speed until blended, about 2 minutes.
4. Stir in chopped nuts.
5. Cover tightly and chill until firm enough to handle, about 30 minutes.
6. Shape into 1-inch balls.
7. Roll in additional confectioners' sugar.
8. Cover tightly and chill at least 2 hours before serving; refrigerate leftovers.

E EASY MARBLED BARS

Yield: about 16 bars

- **15-ounce package sugar cookie mix**
- **5.5-ounce can (½ cup) HERSHEY'S Syrup**

1. Prepare cookie dough according to package directions.
2. Spread in ungreased 8-inch square pan.
3. Pour HERSHEY'S Syrup over top.
4. Use a knife or spatula to lift and swirl batter for a marbled appearance.
5. Bake at 375° for 25 to 30 minutes or until lightly browned.
6. Cool completely before serving.

E CHOCO-COCONUT GOODIES

Yield: about 18 goodies

- **48 vanilla wafer cookies**
- **⅔ cup flaked coconut**
- **⅔ cup unsifted confectioners' sugar**
- **5.5-ounce can (½ cup) HERSHEY'S Syrup**
- **1 teaspoon vanilla**
- **Additional confectioners' sugar**

1. Crush vanilla wafer cookies in blender or food processor to make 1½ cups crumbs.
2. Combine crumbs, coconut and confectioners' sugar in a medium mixing bowl.
3. Stir in HERSHEY'S Syrup and vanilla.
4. Shape into 1-inch balls.
5. Roll in additional confectioners' sugar; refrigerate leftovers.

[M] KID'S SPECIAL COOKIES

Yield: about 30 cookies

18.25 or 18.5-ounce package fudge marble cake mix with chocolate packet
1 egg
⅓ cup vegetable oil
4 tablespoons water
1 cup HERSHEY'S MINI CHIPS

1. Lightly grease a cookie sheet; set aside.
2. Combine dry cake mix, egg, oil and *3 tablespoons* of the water in a large mixer bowl.
3. Beat on medium speed until smooth, about 3 minutes.
4. Stir in HERSHEY'S MINI CHIPS.
5. Measure ⅔ cup batter into small mixer bowl.
6. Blend in chocolate packet from cake mix and remaining 1 tablespoon water; set aside.
7. Drop vanilla MINI CHIP batter by rounded teaspoonfuls onto lightly greased cookie sheet.
8. Drop ½ teaspoonful chocolate batter on top of each cookie.
9. Bake at 350° for 10 to 12 minutes or until very lightly browned.
10. Leave on cookie sheet about 1 minute.
11. Use spatula to remove from cookie sheet.
12. Place on wire rack to cool.

[E] PEANUT BUTTER 'N FUDGE TREATS

Yield: about 24 treats

½ cup butter or margarine
2 cups coarsely broken vanilla wafer cookies
2 cups crisped rice cereal
¾ cup marshmallow creme
⅓ cup HERSHEY'S MINI CHIPS
⅔ cup HERSHEY'S Chocolate Fudge Topping (room temperature)
½ cup REESE'S Peanut Butter Chips

1. Place butter or margarine in a large mixing bowl.
2. Beat with spoon or spatula until softened.
3. Mix in broken vanilla wafers, cereal, marshmallow creme and HERSHEY'S MINI CHIPS.
4. Press mixture into an 8- or 9-inch square pan.
5. Spread HERSHEY'S Chocolate Fudge Topping evenly on top.
6. Sprinkle with REESE'S Peanut Butter Chips.
7. Bake at 325° for 10 minutes.
8. Cool 15 minutes at room temperature.
9. Cover and freeze overnight.
10. Cut into small squares for serving; freeze leftovers.

[E] HIDE AND SEEK COOKIES

Yield: about 32 cookies

17-ounce roll refrigerated sugar cookie dough
8-ounce HERSHEY'S Milk Chocolate Bar
⅔ cup finely chopped nuts

1. Carefully slice cookie dough into ⅜-inch slices.
2. Place on an ungreased cookie sheet.
3. Allow dough to soften at room temperature 5 to 10 minutes.
4. Meanwhile, break HERSHEY'S Milk Chocolate Bar into 32 squares.
5. Place a chocolate square on top of each slice of cookie dough.
6. Shape dough around squares, forming balls which completely cover chocolate.
7. Roll in chopped nuts.
8. Return to ungreased cookie sheet.
9. Bake at 375° for 10 to 12 minutes or until lightly browned.
10. Leave on cookie sheet about 1 minute.
11. Use spatula to remove from cookie sheet.
12. Place on wire rack to cool.

E CHOCOLATE NUT COOKIES   Yield: about 48 cookies

1 ounce (1 block) HERSHEY'S
   Unsweetened Baking Chocolate
2/3 cup sweetened condensed milk
1/4 teaspoon vanilla
2 cups chopped walnuts

1. Lightly grease a cookie sheet; set aside.
2. Melt chocolate in top of double boiler over hot (*not* boiling) water, stirring constantly.*
3. Remove from heat and stir in condensed milk and vanilla.
4. Add chopped nuts and mix well.
5. Drop by rounded teaspoonfuls onto lightly greased cookie sheet.
6. Bake at 350° for 8 to 10 minutes or until set.
7. Use spatula to remove from cookie sheet.
8. Place on wire rack to cool.

*Or, break block of chocolate in half and microwave in a small micro-proof bowl on high (full power) 1 to 1½ minutes or until chocolate is softened; stir to melt and blend.

E CHEWY CHOCOLATE BARS   Yield: about 36 bars

18.25 or 18.5-ounce package yellow
   cake mix
2 eggs
1 cup HERSHEY'S Syrup
1½ cups miniature marshmallows
3/4 cup chopped nuts

1. Grease a 13 x 9-inch pan; set aside.
2. Combine dry cake mix, eggs and HERSHEY'S Syrup in a large mixer bowl.
3. Beat on medium to high speed until blended, about 3 minutes.
4. Stir in marshmallows and nuts.
5. Spread in prepared pan.
6. Bake at 350° for 40 to 45 minutes or until set.
7. Cool completely before serving.

M CHEWY ROLO BROWNIES

Yield: about 36 brownies

36 ROLO pieces
1/4 cup butter or margarine
18.25 or 18.5-ounce package yellow
   cake mix
1/2 cup chopped nuts
5.3-ounce can (2/3 cup) evaporated milk

1. Grease a 13 x 9-inch pan; set aside.
2. Cut ROLO pieces in half crosswise; set aside.
3. Melt butter or margarine in small saucepan over low heat. (Watch carefully.) Set aside.
4. Combine dry cake mix and chopped nuts.
5. Stir in melted butter or margarine and evaporated milk until blended.
6. Spread half (about 1½ cups) of mixture in prepared pan.
7. Bake at 350° for 15 minutes. Remove from oven and immediately place ROLO pieces, cut sides down, onto warm crust.
8. Drop remaining cake mixture by teaspoonfuls evenly over ROLOS in pan. (Do not spread.)
9. Bake at 350° for 25 to 30 minutes or until lightly browned.
10. Cool completely before serving.

E REESE'S PIECES SUGAR COOKIES

Yield: about 36 cookies

15-ounce package sugar cookie mix
1 cup REESE'S PIECES

1. Prepare cookie dough according to package directions.
2. Stir in REESE'S PIECES.
3. Bake according to package directions.

Chewy Rolo Brownies

E EASY PEANUTTY SNICKERDOODLES

Yield: about 30 cookies

- 2 tablespoons sugar
- 2 teaspoons cinnamon
- 15-ounce package sugar cookie mix
- 1 cup REESE'S Peanut Butter Chips

1. Combine sugar and cinnamon in a small mixing bowl; set aside.
2. Prepare cookie dough according to package directions.
3. Stir in REESE'S Peanut Butter Chips.
4. Shape dough into 1-inch balls. (Cover dough and chill about 30 minutes if too soft to handle.)
5. Roll balls in sugar and cinnamon.
6. Place on an ungreased cookie sheet.
7. Bake at 375° for 8 to 10 minutes or until lightly browned.
8. Leave on cookie sheet about 1 minute.
9. Use spatula to remove from cookie sheet.
10. Place on wire rack to cool.

M CHIPPY CHEWY BARS

Yield: about 36 bars

- ½ cup butter or margarine
- 1½ cups graham cracker crumbs
- 12-ounce package (2 cups) HERSHEY'S Semi-Sweet Chocolate Chips
- 1½ cups flaked coconut
- 14-ounce can (1⅓ cups) sweetened condensed milk
- 1½ cups miniature marshmallows

1. Place butter or margarine in a 13 x 9-inch pan.
2. Heat in a 350° oven until melted, about 3 minutes. (Watch carefully.)
3. Remove from oven and sprinkle graham cracker crumbs evenly over melted butter.
4. Press down with fork or spatula.
5. Sprinkle HERSHEY'S Semi-Sweet Chocolate Chips and coconut over crumbs in pan.
6. Drizzle condensed milk evenly over top.
7. Top with miniature marshmallows.
8. Bake at 350° for 20 to 25 minutes or until marshmallows are golden brown.
9. Cool completely before serving.

M S'MORE BARS

Yield: about 24 bars

- ¾ cup butter or margarine
- ⅔ cup sugar
- 1 egg
- 1 teaspoon vanilla
- 3 cups graham cracker crumbs
- ½ cup unsifted all-purpose flour
- ½ teaspoon salt
- 9 1.45-ounce HERSHEY'S Milk Chocolate Bars
- 1 egg white
- 3½ cups miniature marshmallows

1. Grease a 13 x 9-inch pan; set aside.
2. Place butter or margarine in a large mixer bowl.
3. Beat until softened.
4. Add sugar.
5. Beat on medium speed until mixture looks light and fluffy.
6. Blend in egg and vanilla.
7. Stir in graham cracker crumbs, flour and salt.
8. Measure out and set aside 2 cups of the graham cracker crumb mixture.
9. Press remaining mixture into bottom of prepared pan.
10. Place HERSHEY'S Milk Chocolate Bars, side by side, on top of mixture in pan; set aside.
11. Beat egg white with fork until foamy.
12. Stir in marshmallows.
13. Spoon and spread mixture evenly on top of chocolate bars in pan.
14. Press reserved 2 cups graham cracker crumb mixture on top of marshmallows.
15. Bake at 350° for 30 minutes.
16. Cool 10 minutes.
17. Cut into bars.
18. Cool completely before serving.

D PEANUT BUTTER 'N CHOCOLATE BROWNIES

Yield: about 36 brownies

29-ounce roll refrigerated brownie dough
1 cup REESE'S Peanut Butter Chips
3-ounce package cream cheese
¼ cup sugar
1 tablespoon milk
1 egg

1. Grease a 13 x 9-inch pan.
2. Spread brownie dough in prepared pan.
3. Sprinkle *½ cup* of the REESE'S Peanut Butter Chips over dough in pan; set aside.
4. Beat cream cheese on medium speed in small mixer bowl until softened, about 1 minute.
5. Add sugar and beat well, about 2 minutes; set aside.
6. Melt remaining ½ cup peanut butter chips with milk in top of double boiler over hot (*not* boiling) water, stirring constantly until blended.
7. Add melted peanut butter chip mixture *while warm* to cream cheese mixture.
8. Beat on medium to high speed until smooth and fluffy, about 2 minutes.
9. Add egg and beat well.
10. Place heaping tablespoonfuls of peanut butter mixture on top of brownie dough in pan.
11. Use knife or spatula to lift and swirl dough. (Dough will be stiff.)
12. Bake at 350° for 35 to 40 minutes or until golden brown.
13. Cool completely before serving.

E CHUNKY CHOCOLATE COOKIES

Yield: about 10 big cookies

15-ounce package sugar cookie mix
8-ounce HERSHEY'S Milk Chocolate Bar or SPECIAL DARK Bar

1. Prepare cookie dough according to package directions; set aside.
2. Break HERSHEY'S Milk Chocolate Bar or SPECIAL DARK Bar into 32 squares.
3. Cut each square into 4 pieces or "chunks."
4. Stir chunks into cookie dough.
5. Drop by ¼ cupfuls* 2 inches apart on an ungreased cookie sheet.
6. Bake at 375° for 12 to 14 minutes or until *very* lightly browned.
7. Leave on cookie sheet about 1 minute.
8. Use spatula to remove from cookie sheet.
9. Place on wire rack to cool.

*An ice cream scoop that equals ¼ cup may be used to drop cookies.

M SECRET KISS COOKIES

Yield: about 36 cookies

1 cup butter or margarine
½ cup sugar
1 teaspoon vanilla
1¾ cups unsifted all-purpose flour
1 cup finely chopped walnuts
36 HERSHEY'S KISSES
Confectioners' sugar

1. Place butter or margarine in a large mixer bowl.
2. Beat until softened.
3. Add sugar and vanilla.
4. Beat on medium speed until mixture looks light and fluffy.
5. Gradually add flour and nuts.
6. Beat on low speed after each addition until well blended.
7. Cover bowl tightly and chill 1 hour.
8. Shape about 1 tablespoon of dough around each HERSHEY'S KISS. (Be sure KISS is completely covered with dough.)
9. Place on an ungreased cookie sheet.
10. Bake at 375° for 10 to 12 minutes or until set.
11. Leave on cookie sheet about 1 minute.
12. Use spatula to remove from cookie sheet.
13. Roll in confectioners' sugar while warm.
14. Place on wire rack to cool.
15. Roll in confectioners' sugar again just before serving.

Place Your Order Here

 COOKIE BURGERS

Yield: about 16 cookies

12-ounce package (2 cups) REESE'S
Peanut Butter Chips
15-ounce package sugar cookie mix
½ cup flaked coconut
2 to 3 drops green food color
Cocoa Filling (recipe follows)

1. Chop REESE'S Peanut Butter Chips in nut chopper or by hand. (Do *not* use blender or food processor.) Set aside.
2. Prepare cookie dough according to package directions.
3. Stir in *1 cup* of the chopped peanut butter chips.
4. Shape into 1¼-inch balls. (Cover dough and chill about 30 minutes if too soft to handle.)
5. Place 2 inches apart on an ungreased cookie sheet.
6. Gently press a few of the remaining chopped peanut butter chips onto top of each unbaked cookie.
7. Bake at 375° for 8 to 10 minutes or until *very* lightly browned.
8. Leave on cookie sheet about 1 minute.
9. Use spatula to remove from cookie sheet.
10. Place on wire rack to cool.
11. Toss coconut with green food color to look like "relish"; set aside.
12. Frost bottoms of half the amount of cookies with 3 level tablespoons of Cocoa Filling to look like "burgers."
13. Sprinkle with green coconut.
14. Gently press unfilled cookie on top to form "bun."

Cocoa Filling

½ cup butter or margarine
½ cup HERSHEY'S Cocoa
2⅔ cups unsifted confectioners' sugar
¼ cup milk
1 teaspoon vanilla

1. Beat butter or margarine on medium speed in large mixer bowl until softened, about 1 minute.
2. Add HERSHEY'S Cocoa, confectioners' sugar, milk and vanilla.
3. Beat on low speed until ingredients are moistened.
4. Beat on medium speed until blended and creamy, about 3 minutes.

 GRILLED CHOCOLATE SANDWICH

Yield: 1 sandwich

2 slices any flavor bread
Soft butter or margarine
1 to 2 1.45-ounce HERSHEY'S Milk Chocolate Bars

1. Spread soft butter or margarine on one side of each bread slice.
2. Place HERSHEY'S Milk Chocolate Bars between bread slices, buttered sides *out*.
3. Grill *slowly* on both sides until chocolate has melted and bread is golden brown.
4. Serve warm.

Variations—add sliced fresh strawberries or peanut butter with chocolate before grilling.

PEANUTTY FRIES

Yield: about 40 fries

> **12-ounce package (2 cups) REESE'S Peanut Butter Chips**
> **14-ounce can (1⅓ cups) sweetened condensed milk**

1. Butter an 8- or 9-inch square pan; set aside.
2. Combine REESE'S Peanut Butter Chips and condensed milk in large microproof bowl.
3. Microwave on high (full power) for 1½ minutes or until chips are softened.
4. Stir until chips are melted and blended. (If necessary, microwave on high a few additional seconds to melt chips.)*
5. Pat mixture into prepared pan.
6. Cool completely at room temperature.
7. Cut into strips to look like french fries.
8. Carefully remove with metal spatula or table knife.

*Or, melt and blend in top of double boiler over hot water.

 DOUBLE CHOCOLATE SHAKE

Yield: 1 serving

> **½ cup HERSHEY'S Chocolate Milk**
> **1 cup (3 to 4 large scoops) chocolate ice cream**

1. Place HERSHEY'S Chocolate Milk in blender container.
2. Add ice cream.
3. Cover and blend on medium to high speed until thick and smooth.
4. Adjust milk or ice cream levels to suit taste.
5. Serve immediately.

Prepare to assemble "burgers."

Frost bottoms of half of the cookies with Cocoa Filling.

Sprinkle with "relish." Gently press unfilled cookie on top to form "bun."

D SUNDAE PIZZA

Yield: 10 to 12 wedges

> ¾ cup shortening
> 1 cup packed light brown sugar
> 1 egg
> 2¼ cups unsifted all-purpose flour
> ¼ teaspoon baking soda
> ¼ teaspoon cinnamon
> ¼ teaspoon salt
> 5.5-ounce can (½ cup) HERSHEY'S Syrup
> 1 quart any flavor ice cream
> Sliced fresh fruits (bananas, strawberries, pineapple or other)
> Chocolate Caramel Ice Cream Sauce (page 63)

1. Cream shortening and brown sugar until light and fluffy in a large mixer bowl.
2. Blend in egg on medium speed.
3. In a separate bowl, combine flour, baking soda, cinnamon and salt.
4. Blend about a third of the flour mixture into the creamed mixture.
5. Blend in about ¼ cup of the HERSHEY'S Syrup.
6. Add another third of the flour mixture, then remaining syrup.
7. Blend in remaining flour, beating well on medium speed.
8. Pat dough evenly into a greased 12-inch pizza pan, making a 1-inch wide edge inside rim of pan.
9. Bake at 375° for 10 to 12 minutes or until top springs back when lightly touched.
10. Cool completely.
11. Cut into 10 or 12 pizza-shaped wedges.
12. Place a small scoop of ice cream on each wedge.
13. Freeze until firm.
14. Wrap and continue freezing until ready to serve.
15. Place "pizza" wedges on serving plates.
16. Arrange sliced fruits around ice cream on wedges.
17. Top with Chocolate Caramel Ice Cream Sauce.
18. Serve immediately.

COOKIE ICE CREAM BALLS

Yield: 8 balls

> 10 chocolate sandwich cookies
> ½ gallon vanilla ice cream
> Peanut Butter Sauce (recipe follows)

1. Line a cookie sheet with wax paper.
2. Place in freezer.
3. Crush chocolate sandwich cookies (filling included) in blender or food processor to make 1 cup crumbs; set aside.
4. Make eight 2½-inch diameter ice cream balls using large scoop.
5. Roll in crumbs.
6. Place on cold wax paper-lined cookie sheet.
7. Cover and freeze while preparing Peanut Butter Sauce.
8. Serve each with about ¼ cup warm sauce.

Peanut Butter Sauce

> 12-ounce package (2 cups) REESE'S Peanut Butter Chips
> ⅔ cup milk
> ½ cup heavy (whipping) cream
> ¼ teaspoon vanilla

1. Melt REESE'S Peanut Butter Chips with milk and heavy cream in medium saucepan, stirring constantly over low heat until blended.
2. Remove from heat and stir in vanilla.

CHOCOLATE SYRUP SODA

Yield: 1 serving

- ¼ **cup cold club soda**
- 3 **tablespoons HERSHEY'S Syrup**
- 2 **small scoops vanilla ice cream**
  Additional club soda
  Whipped topping and maraschino cherry

1. Combine club soda and HERSHEY'S Syrup in a tall glass.
2. Add ice cream.
3. Fill glass with additional club soda.
4. Stir slightly.
5. Top with whipped topping and a maraschino cherry.
6. Serve immediately.

Double Chocolate Soda: Use 2 small scoops of chocolate ice cream in place of vanilla ice cream.

 ## FUDGEY FREEZER POPS

Yield: 5 pops

- 1 **envelope whipped topping mix (to yield 2 cups topping)**
- ¾ **cup HERSHEY'S Chocolate Fudge Topping (room temperature)**
- 2 **tablespoons water**
- 5 **popsicle sticks**
  Cookie crumbs, crushed cereal or chopped nuts

1. Prepare whipped topping mix according to package directions.
2. Fold in HERSHEY'S Chocolate Fudge Topping and water.
3. Spoon into five 5-ounce paper drink cups.
4. Insert popsicle stick into center of each pop.
5. Cover and freeze overnight.
6. Carefully peel off cups.
7. Roll pops in cookie crumbs, crushed cereal or chopped nuts to coat.
8. Serve immediately.

M CHOCOLATE CRUMB SANDWICH SQUARES

Yield: about 16 squares

- ½ **cup butter or margarine**
- ½ **cup packed light brown sugar**
- 1½ **cups graham cracker crumbs**
  8-ounce HERSHEY'S Milk Chocolate Bar with Almonds

1. Grease an 8-inch square pan; set aside.
2. Melt butter or margarine with brown sugar in a small saucepan over medium heat, stirring occasionally to blend.
3. Remove from heat and stir in graham cracker crumbs until thoroughly moistened.
4. Measure out 1 cup crumb mixture; set aside.
5. Press remaining crumb mixture into prepared pan; set aside.
6. Melt HERSHEY'S Milk Chocolate Bar with Almonds in top of double boiler over hot (*not* boiling) water, stirring constantly until smooth.
7. Spread melted chocolate evenly over crumb mixture in pan.
8. Press reserved 1 cup crumb mixture on top.
9. Cool to room temperature.
10. Cover and chill overnight before serving.
11. Store in a cool, dry place.

Overleaf: Sundae Pizza, 36; Cookie Burgers, 34; Peanutty Fries, 35; Double Chocolate Shake, 35

Mother Nature's Best

The recipes in this section feature HERSHEY'S and REESE'S products combined with nuts, fruits, grains, and dairy products. Nuts, fruits, grains, and dairy products supply valuable protein, vitamins, and minerals. By adding these to your favorite recipes, you will increase their nutritional content. Combine them with the nutrients in HERSHEY'S chocolate products and REESE'S Peanut Butter Chips, and you will have a nutritious, high-energy snack.

SPICY CHOCOLATE EGGNOG

Yield: about 4 servings

- **4 eggs**
- **2 cups milk**
- **1 cup heavy (whipping) cream**
- **5.5-ounce can (½ cup) HERSHEY'S Syrup**
- **½ cup unsifted confectioners' sugar**
- **⅛ teaspoon cinnamon**
- **⅛ teaspoon nutmeg**

1. Place all ingredients in blender container.
2. Cover and blend on low speed until blended.
3. Cover and chill until ready to serve.

PEANUTTY APPLE DROPS

Yield: about 48 cookies

- **½ cup butter or margarine**
- **1¼ cups packed light brown sugar**
- **1 egg**
- **¼ cup apple juice**
- **2 cups unsifted all-purpose flour**
- **1 teaspoon baking soda**
- **¼ teaspoon salt**
- **1 cup REESE'S Peanut Butter Chips**
- **1 cup finely chopped apple (with or without peel)**
- **1 cup raisins**

1. Lightly grease cookie sheet; set aside.
2. Place butter or margarine in a large mixer bowl.
3. Beat until softened.
4. Add brown sugar.
5. Beat on medium speed until mixture looks lighter and fluffy.
6. Blend in egg and apple juice.
7. In a separate bowl, combine flour, baking soda and salt.
8. Add to butter-sugar mixture.
9. Beat on low speed until ingredients are moistened.
10. Beat on medium speed until blended and smooth, about 2 minutes.
11. Stir in REESE'S Peanut Butter Chips, apple and raisins.
12. Drop by rounded teaspoonfuls onto lightly greased cookie sheet.
13. Bake at 375° for 8 to 10 minutes or until lightly browned.
14. Leave on cookie sheet about 1 minute.
15. Use spatula to remove from cookie sheet.
16. Place on wire rack to cool.

M CHOCK-FULL BROWNIES

Yield: about 16 brownies

- 1½ **cups graham cracker crumbs**
- ⅓ **cup HERSHEY'S Cocoa**
- 14-ounce **can (1⅓ cups) sweetened condensed milk**
- 1 **tablespoon honey**
- 2 **tablespoons orange juice**
- 1 **cup REESE'S Peanut Butter Chips**
- ½ **cup raisins**
- ½ **cup chopped nuts**

1. Grease a 9-inch square pan; set aside.
2. Combine graham cracker crumbs and HERSHEY'S Cocoa in a medium mixing bowl.
3. Add remaining ingredients.
4. Stir until thoroughly combined.
5. Pour into prepared pan.
6. Bake at 350° for 25 to 30 minutes or until brownie begins to pull away from sides of pan.
7. Cool about 15 minutes.
8. Cut into bars.
9. Serve warm or cool.

M COCOA PEANUTTY CRUNCH SQUARES

Yield: about 16 squares

- ½ **cup peanut butter**
- ¼ **cup HERSHEY'S Cocoa**
- ½ **cup sugar**
- ½ **cup light corn syrup or honey**
- 2 **cups bite-size honey graham cereal**
- 1 **cup granola**
- ¼ **cup raisins**

1. Butter an 8-inch square pan; set aside.
2. Combine peanut butter and HERSHEY'S Cocoa in a small mixing bowl; set aside.
3. Combine sugar and corn syrup or honey in a medium saucepan.
4. Stir constantly over medium heat until mixture boils.
5. Boil and stir 1 minute.
6. Remove from heat and stir in chocolate-peanut butter mixture.
7. Stir in cereal, granola and raisins.
8. Spread mixture in prepared pan.
9. Cool completely before serving.
10. Store in a cool, dry place.

M PEANUTTY APPLE CRISP

Yield: about 6 servings

- **About 6 medium apples**
- ¾ **cup packed light brown sugar**
- ½ **cup unsifted all-purpose flour**
- ½ **cup quick-cooking oats**
- ½ **teaspoon cinnamon**
- ½ **teaspoon nutmeg**
- ⅓ **cup butter or margarine**
- 1 **cup REESE'S Peanut Butter Chips**
- **Vanilla ice cream or whipped topping**

1. Grease a 9-inch square pan; set aside.
2. Peel and slice apples to make 4 cups.
3. Place in prepared pan; set aside.
4. Combine brown sugar, flour, oats, cinnamon and nutmeg in a small mixing bowl.
5. Cut butter or margarine into sugar-oat mixture with fork or pastry cutter to form coarse crumbs.
6. Stir in REESE'S Peanut Butter Chips.
7. Sprinkle evenly over apple slices in pan.
8. Bake at 375° for 25 to 30 minutes or until golden brown.
9. Serve warm with ice cream or whipped topping.

[M] NO-BAKE PEANUT BUTTER CRUNCHIES

Yield: about 16 squares

5 cups whole wheat or corn flakes
12-ounce package (2 cups) REESE'S Peanut Butter Chips
1 tablespoon shortening (*not* butter, margarine or oil)
1 cup raisins

1. Butter an 8-inch square pan; set aside.
2. Coarsely crush whole wheat or corn flakes with rolling pin; set aside.
3. Melt REESE'S Peanut Butter Chips with shortening in top of double boiler over hot (*not* boiling) water, stirring constantly until blended.
4. Remove from heat and stir in crushed corn flakes and raisins until thoroughly coated with peanut butter mixture.
5. Press into prepared pan.
6. Let stand at room temperature 30 minutes.
7. Cut into squares.
8. Cool completely before serving.
9. Store in a cool, dry place.

[M] PEANUT BUTTER FONDUE

Yield: about 4 cups fondue

Selection of fruits and other fondue dippers
2 12-ounce packages (4 cups) REESE'S Peanut Butter Chips
1 pint light cream

1. Prepare ahead of time a selection of fresh or canned, well-drained fruit chunks for dipping: apples, bananas, pears, peaches, cherries, pineapple, oranges. (Brush fresh fruits with lemon juice to prevent browning.) Cover and chill until ready to serve. Marshmallows and bite-size pieces of pound cake also make super fondue dippers!
2. Melt REESE'S Peanut Butter Chips with light cream in top of double boiler over hot (*not* boiling) water, stirring constantly until blended.
3. Pour into a medium fondue pot. (Keep warm over low heat source.)
4. Dip chunks of fruit, cake and marshmallows into warm fondue with forks. (Leftover fondue may be reheated in top of double boiler over hot water and used as an ice cream sauce.)

E CHOCOLATE BANANA SHAKE

Yield: about 2 servings

- **1 small ripe banana**
- **1 cup milk**
- **⅓ cup HERSHEY'S Chocolate Fudge Topping (room temperature)**
- **4 large scoops vanilla ice cream**

1. Slice banana into blender container.
2. Add *½ cup* of the milk.
3. Cover and blend on high speed until smoot
4. Add HERSHEY'S Chocolate Fudge Toppin remaining milk and ice cream.
5. Cover and blend on high speed until thi and smooth.
6. Serve immediately.

M PEANUTTY BANANA POPS

Yield: 8 pops

- **4 medium bananas**
- **8 popsicle sticks**
- **1 cup REESE'S Peanut Butter Chips**
- **1 tablespoon vegetable oil**
  Finely chopped nuts

1. Cut bananas in half crosswise.
2. Insert popsicle stick in cut end of each half.
3. Wrap and freeze at least 4 hours.
4. Combine REESE'S Peanut Butter Chips and oil in small, heavy skillet.
5. Stir constantly over *very low* heat until chips are melted and blended; remove from heat.
6. Quickly dip frozen banana half into war peanut butter chip mixture, twirling to r move excess coating. (If coating thicker reheat over low heat with a few addition drops oil.)
7. Immediately roll in chopped nuts.
8. Repeat steps 6 and 7 until all pops a coated.
9. Cover and freeze at least one hour befo serving. (Leftovers can be wrapped and fr zen up to 3 days.)

E MINI CHIP TRAIL MIX

- **1 cup HERSHEY'S MINI CHIPS**
- **½ cup salted sunflower kernels**
- **½ cup dry roasted peanuts**
- **½ cup raisins**

Yield: about 2 cups

1. Toss ingredients together in small bowl.
2. Store in air-tight container.

PEANUT BUTTER TARTS

Yield: 6 tarts

**3.5-ounce package instant vanilla pudding
and pie filling mix**
1½ cups cold milk
1 cup REESE'S Peanut Butter Chips
**4-ounce package (6) tart-size graham
cracker crumb crusts**
Whipped topping and sliced fresh fruit

1. Combine pudding mix with *1 cup* of the milk
in a small mixer bowl.
2. Beat on low speed 2 minutes; set aside.
3. Melt REESE'S Peanut Butter Chips with remaining ½ cup milk in top of double boiler
over hot (*not* boiling) water, stirring constantly until blended.
4. Gradually add peanut butter mixture *while
warm* to pudding, beating well on low speed
after each addition.
5. Beat mixture on medium to high speed an
additional minute.
6. Spoon into tart crusts.
7. Serve immediately or cover and chill.
8. Top with whipped topping and sliced fresh
fruit just before serving; refrigerate leftovers.

 FRUIT AND NUT BARS

Yield: about 24 cookies

½ cup butter or margarine
1 cup packed light brown sugar
1 egg
1 teaspoon vanilla
1½ cups unsifted all-purpose flour
½ teaspoon baking powder
½ teaspoon salt
¼ teaspoon cinnamon
1 cup HERSHEY'S MINI CHIPS
½ cup raisins
½ cup chopped dried apricots
½ cup chopped pitted prunes
½ cup chopped pecans
MINI CHIP Marshmallow Glaze (page 60)

1. Grease a 13 x 9-inch pan; set aside.
2. Place butter or margarine in a large mixer
bowl.
3. Beat until softened.
4. Add brown sugar.
5. Beat on medium speed until mixture looks
lighter and fluffy.
6. Blend in egg and vanilla.
7. In a separate bowl, combine flour, baking
powder, salt and cinnamon.
8. Add to butter-sugar mixture.
9. Beat on low speed until ingredients are
moistened.
10. Beat on medium speed until blended and
smooth, about 2 minutes.
11. Stir in HERSHEY'S MINI CHIPS, raisins,
chopped apricots, prunes and pecans.
12. Spread in prepared pan.
13. Bake at 375° for 25 to 30 minutes or until
lightly browned.
14. Cool completely.
15. Glaze with MINI CHIP Marshmallow Glaze.
16. Allow Glaze to set before serving.

E CHOCOBERRY SPLASH

Yield: 1 serving

- ¾ cup skim milk or 2% milk
- 3 tablespoons frozen strawberries with syrup, thawed
- 2 tablespoons HERSHEY'S Syrup
- 1 small scoop vanilla ice cream
  Crushed ice
- 1 to 2 tablespoons club soda
  Vanilla ice cream and additional fruit

1. Combine milk, strawberries, HERSHEY'S Syrup and ice cream in blender container.
2. Cover and blend on medium speed until smooth.
3. Pour into a glass filled with crushed ice.
4. Add a splash club soda.
5. Stir slightly.
6. Top with a scoop of vanilla ice cream and fresh fruit.
7. Serve immediately.

Fruit Variations — Substitute any of the following for the strawberries:

Peach — ⅓ cup canned peach slices or one canned peach half, drained

Raspberry — 3 tablespoons frozen raspberries with syrup, thawed

Pineapple — 2 slices canned or ¼ cup crushed pineapple, drained

M STRAWBERRY COCOA MOUSSE

Yield: about 4 servings

- 10-ounce package frozen strawberries, thawed
- ¼ cup cold water
- 1 envelope unflavored gelatine
- ½ cup milk
- ⅓ cup HERSHEY'S Cocoa
- ¼ cup sugar
- ½ teaspoon vanilla
- 1 cup heavy (whipping) cream
  Fresh strawberries
  Sliced almonds

1. Drain strawberries, reserving 3 tablespoons of the syrup; set aside.
2. Combine water and gelatine in blender container.
3. Let stand 5 minutes to soften gelatine.
4. Meanwhile, heat milk in small saucepan until hot but *not* boiling.
5. Add to gelatine in blender.
6. Cover and blend on medium speed until gelatine is dissolved.
7. Add HERSHEY'S Cocoa and sugar.
8. Cover and blend on medium speed.
9. Add strawberries, reserved strawberry syrup and vanilla.
10. Cover and blend well.
11. Add heavy cream.
12. Cover and blend.
13. Pour into dessert dishes.
14. Cover and chill overnight.
15. Top with fresh strawberries and sliced almonds just before serving.

Chocoberry Splash, this page
Peanut Butter Tarts, 45

Candy Bar Express

 HERSHEY BAR MOUSSE

Yield: about 6 servings

> 2 eggs
> 8-ounce HERSHEY'S Milk Chocolate Bar
> ¼ cup water
> 1 cup heavy (whipping) cream

1. Beat eggs with fork or rotary beater; set aside.
2. Break HERSHEY'S Milk Chocolate Bar into pieces and place in a medium micro-proof bowl.
3. Add water.
4. Microwave on high (full power) for 1½ to 2 minutes or until chocolate is softened.
5. Stir until chocolate is melted and blended. (If necessary, microwave on high a few additional seconds to melt chocolate.)
6. Stir in beaten eggs.
7. Microwave on medium (½ power) for 1½ to 2½ minutes or until mixture is hot, but not boiling.
8. Cool 5 minutes.
9. Beat heavy cream until stiff.
10. Fold in chocolate mixture.
11. Pour into an 8-inch square pan.
12. Cover and freeze overnight.
13. Cut into squares to serve.

 GOOD BARS

Yield: about 24 bars

> 24 vanilla wafer cookies
> ¼ cup butter or margarine
> ⅔ cup flaked coconut
> 8-ounce HERSHEY'S MR. GOODBAR Chocolate Bar
> ¾ cup sweetened condensed milk

1. Crush vanilla wafer cookies in blender or food processor to make ¾ cup crumbs; set aside.
2. Place butter or margarine in an 8-inch square pan.
3. Heat in a 350° oven until melted, about 1 minute. (Watch carefully.)
4. Remove from oven and sprinkle vanilla wafer crumbs evenly over melted butter.
5. Sprinkle coconut over crumbs; set aside.
6. Break HERSHEY'S MR. GOODBAR Chocolate Bar into pieces.
7. Melt with condensed milk in top of double boiler over hot (*not* boiling) water, stirring constantly until blended.
8. Carefully spoon chocolate mixture over coconut in pan.
9. Spread evenly.
10. Bake at 350° for 30 minutes.
11. Cool overnight before serving.

CANDY BAR MARBLED CAKE

Yield: about 8 servings

16-ounce package pound cake mix
¾ cup chopped nuts
8-ounce HERSHEY'S Milk Chocolate Bar
3 tablespoons milk
Confectioners' sugar

1. Grease a 9 x 5-inch loaf pan and line bottom with wax paper; set aside.
2. Prepare cake batter according to package directions.
3. Stir in chopped nuts.
4. Measure out 1 cup of the batter; set aside.
5. Pour remaining batter into prepared pan; set aside.
6. Break HERSHEY'S Milk Chocolate Bar into pieces.
7. Melt chocolate with milk in top of double boiler over hot (*not* boiling) water, stirring constantly until blended.
8. Stir melted chocolate *while warm* into reserved 1 cup cake batter until blended.
9. Place heaping tablespoonfuls of chocolate batter on top of cake batter in pan.
10. Use a knife or spatula to lift and swirl batter for a marbled appearance.
11. Bake at 325° for 55 to 65 minutes or until cake tester inserted comes out clean.
12. Cool 10 to 15 minutes in pan.
13. Carefully run a knife along sides of pan to loosen cake.
14. Remove cake from pan onto wire rack to cool completely.
15. Sprinkle with confectioners' sugar just before serving.

CHEWY DARK CHOCOLATE TREATS

Yield: about 24 treats

2 cups crisped rice cereal
¾ cup coarsely chopped pretzels
1 cup chopped unsalted peanuts
8-ounce HERSHEY'S SPECIAL DARK Bar
1 cup marshmallow creme
2 tablespoons butter or margarine
2 tablespoons milk
1 teaspoon vanilla

1. Line a 9-inch square pan with foil.
2. Lightly butter foil; set aside.
3. Mix cereal, chopped pretzels and peanuts in a large mixing bowl; set aside.
4. Break HERSHEY'S SPECIAL DARK Bar into pieces.
5. Melt chocolate with marshmallow creme, butter or margarine and milk in a medium saucepan over low to medium heat, stirring constantly until blended.
6. Continue stirring constantly over low to medium heat 3 additional minutes.
7. Remove from heat and add vanilla.
8. Add chocolate mixture to cereal mixture.
9. Stir until cereal, pretzels and peanuts are well coated with chocolate mixture.
10. Quickly press mixture into prepared pan.
11. Cover and chill at least 45 minutes.
12. Cut into small squares for serving; refrigerate leftovers.

Overleaf: Hershey Bar Fondue;
Chocolate Bar Croissants;
Candy Bar Marbled Cake, this page

CHOCOLATE BAR CROISSANTS

Yield: 8 croissants

8-ounce roll refrigerated crescent dinner roll dough

2 1.45-ounce HERSHEY'S Milk Chocolate Bars

1. Separate dough into 8 triangles.
2. Break each HERSHEY'S Milk Chocolate Bar into 12 pieces.
3. Place 2 pieces of the chocolate bar side by side at wide end of each triangle.
4. Place 1 additional piece on top.
5. Starting at wide end, roll dough to opposite point.
6. Pinch edges together to cover and seal chocolate.
7. Place rolls, pointed side down, on an ungreased baking sheet.
8. Bake at 375° for 8 to 10 minutes or until lightly browned.
9. Leave on cookie sheet about 1 minute.
10. Use spatula to remove from cookie sheet.
11. Place on wire rack to cool about 10 minutes.
12. Serve warm.

M HERSHEY BAR FONDUE

Yield: about 2½ cups fondue

Selection of fruits and other fondue dippers
2 8-ounce HERSHEY'S Milk Chocolate Bars
4-ounce HERSHEY'S SPECIAL DARK Bar
5.3-ounce can (⅔ cup) evaporated milk
½ teaspoon almond extract

1. Prepare ahead of time a selection of fresh or canned, well-drained fruit chunks for dipping: apples, bananas, pears, peaches, cherries, pineapple, oranges. (Brush fresh fruit with lemon juice to prevent browning.) Cover and chill until ready to serve. Marshmallows and bite-size pieces of pound cake also make super fondue dippers!

2. Break HERSHEY'S Milk Chocolate Bars and SPECIAL DARK Bar into pieces and place in a medium micro-proof bowl.
3. Add evaporated milk.
4. Microwave on high (full power) for 1½ to 2 minutes or until chocolate is softened.
5. Stir until chocolate is melted and blended. (If necessary, microwave on high a few additional minutes to melt chocolate.)
6. Stir in almond extract.
7. Pour into a medium fondue pot. (Keep warm over low heat source.)
8. Dip chunks of fruit, cake and marshmallows into warm fondue with forks.

Best-ever Special Occasion Favorites

E CUPID'S CHOCOLATE PUDDING

Yield: about 6 servings

4⅛-ounce package instant chocolate pudding and pie filling mix
2 cups (1 pint) HERSHEY'S Chocolate Milk
Whipped topping and red candy hearts

1. Prepare pudding according to package directions, using HERSHEY'S Chocolate Milk in place of white milk.
2. Cover and chill until ready to serve.
3. Top with whipped topping and candy hearts just before serving; refrigerate leftovers.

E DOUBLE CHOCOLATE SWEETHEART PIE

Yield: about 6 servings

4⅛-ounce package instant chocolate pudding and pie filling mix
1¾ cups HERSHEY'S Chocolate Milk
6-ounce packaged graham cracker pie crust
Whipped topping

1. Prepare pie filling according to package directions, using HERSHEY'S Chocolate Milk in place of white milk.
2. Pour into crust.
3. Cover and chill overnight.
4. Serve with whipped topping; refrigerate leftovers.

M GOBLIN CHIPCAKES

Yield: about 36 cupcakes

> 8-ounce package cream cheese
> 1 egg
> ⅓ cup sugar
> ⅛ teaspoon salt
> 3 drops red food color
> 3 drops yellow food color
> 5.75-ounce package (1 cup) HERSHEY'S Milk Chocolate Chips
> 18.25 or 18.5-ounce package devil's food cake mix

1. Place paper liners in 2½-inch muffin cups; set aside.
2. Beat cream cheese on medium speed in small mixer bowl until softened, about 1 minute.
3. Add egg, sugar, salt and food colors.
4. Beat on medium speed until blended, about 2 minutes.
5. Stir in HERSHEY'S Milk Chocolate Chips; set aside.
6. Prepare cake batter according to package directions.
7. Fill paper-lined muffin cups *half* full with batter.
8. Spoon one level tablespoonful of cream cheese-chocolate chip mixture on top of each cupcake.
9. Bake at 350° for 25 to 30 minutes or until very lightly browned.
10. Cool. (No need to frost.)

E BUNNY FUDGE BITS

Yield: about 42 pieces

> 1 cup HERSHEY'S Chocolate Fudge Topping (room temperature)
> ½ cup extra crunchy peanut butter
> 1 cup flaked coconut
> Chopped peanuts or graham cracker crumbs

1. Combine HERSHEY'S Chocolate Fudge Topping, peanut butter and coconut with spoon in medium mixing bowl.
2. Cover and chill 30 minutes.
3. Shape mixture into ¾-inch balls.
4. Roll in chopped peanuts or graham cracker crumbs.
5. Cover and chill until ready to serve; refrigerate leftovers.

E EASY PARTY PARFAITS

Yield: 6 parfaits

> 4⅛-ounce package instant chocolate pudding and pie filling mix
> 2 cups (1 pint) HERSHEY'S Chocolate Milk
> 2½ cups non-dairy whipped topping, thawed
> 6 maraschino cherries, well drained

1. Prepare pudding according to package directions, using HERSHEY'S Chocolate Milk in place of white milk.
2. Alternate pudding with about 2 cups of the whipped topping in 6 parfait glasses, beginning and ending with pudding.
3. Serve immediately or cover and chill.
4. Top with remaining whipped topping and drained maraschino cherries just before serving; refrigerate leftovers.

MINI CHIP PARTY TARTS

Yield: about 24 tarts

- **24 vanilla wafer cookies**
- **2 8-ounce packages cream cheese**
- **½ cup sugar**
- **2 eggs**
- **½ teaspoon vanilla**
- **1 cup HERSHEY'S MINI CHIPS**
- **21-ounce can cherry pie filling**

1. Place paper liners in 2½-inch muffin cups.
2. Place one vanilla wafer cookie (flat side down) into the bottom of each cup; set aside.
3. Beat cream cheese on medium speed in large mixer bowl until softened, about 1 minute.
4. Add sugar, eggs and vanilla.
5. Beat on medium to high speed until blended and smooth, about 2 minutes.
6. Stir in HERSHEY'S MINI CHIPS.
7. Spoon a rounded tablespoonful of the cream cheese mixture on top of each cookie in paper-lined cups.
8. Bake at 350° for 30 to 35 minutes or until set, but not browned.
9. Cool completely.
10. Cover and chill at least 3 hours before serving.
11. Top each tart with a rounded tablespoonful of cherry pie filling just before serving; refrigerate leftovers.

Prepare muffin cups and place vanilla wafer in each paper liner.

Spoon cream cheese mixture on top of cookie.

Top each tart with cherry pie filling.

Peanut Butter Party Cones, 57
MINI CHIP Party Tarts, this page
Easy Party Parfaits, 53

MOM'S DAY CHOCOLATE PIE

Yield: about 6 servings

 2 egg yolks
⅓ cup cornstarch
¼ teaspoon salt
1¾ cups milk
 1 cup HERSHEY'S Syrup
 1 teaspoon vanilla
 6-ounce packaged graham cracker
   pie crust
   Whipped topping

1. Beat egg yolks with fork or rotary beater in a medium micro-proof bowl.
2. Add cornstarch, salt, milk and HERSHEY'S Syrup.
3. Mix well.
4. Microwave on medium-high (⅔ power) for 6 to 8 minutes, stirring every 2 minutes with wire whisk until mixture is smooth and thickened.
5. Stir in vanilla.
6. Pour into crust.
7. Place plastic wrap directly onto surface of pie.
8. Chill overnight.
9. Serve with whipped topping.

M CREME-FILLED PARTY CUPCAKES

Yield: about 24 cupcakes

18.25 or 18.5-ounce package yellow or
   chocolate cake mix
 2 3-ounce packages cream cheese
 1 cup HERSHEY'S Chocolate Fudge
   Topping (room temperature)
 1 teaspoon vanilla
   Dash salt

1. Prepare cake batter and bake according to package directions for cupcakes; set aside to cool completely.
2. Meanwhile, beat cream cheese on medium speed in small mixer bowl until softened about 1 minute.
3. Add HERSHEY'S Chocolate Fudge Topping vanilla and salt.
4. Beat on medium speed until well blended about 2 minutes.
5. Cut a 1-inch wide and ½-inch deep cone from top of each cupcake.
6. Fill each hole with about 1 tablespoon topping mixture.
7. Cover and chill until ready to serve; refrigerate leftovers.

YANKEE DOODLE FREEZER PIE

Yield: about 6 servings

 8-ounce container (3½ cups) frozen
   non-dairy whipped topping, thawed
 1 cup HERSHEY'S Chocolate Fudge
   Topping (room temperature)
¼ cup milk
 6-ounce package chocolate flavor pie crust
   Additional HERSHEY'S Chocolate Fudge
   Topping, warmed
   Miniature red, white and blue flags

1. Combine whipped topping, HERSHEY'S Chocolate Fudge Topping and milk in small mixer bowl.
2. Beat on low speed until blended, about minute.
3. Spoon into pie crust.
4. Cover and freeze overnight.
5. Serve with additional warm fudge topping and decorate with miniature flags.

M FESTIVE CREAM-FILLED POUND CAKE

Yield: about 8 servings

10.75-ounce frozen pound cake, thawed
1 cup heavy (whipping) cream
Dash salt
½ teaspoon almond extract
½ cup HERSHEY'S Chocolate Fudge Topping (room temperature)
Additional HERSHEY'S Chocolate Fudge Topping and sliced almonds

1. Cut cake horizontally into 4 thin layers; set aside.
2. Combine heavy cream, salt and almond extract in a small mixer bowl.
3. Beat on high speed until stiff.
4. Fold in HERSHEY'S Chocolate Fudge Topping.
5. Spread each cake layer with about ¼ cup of the fudge-cream mixture.
6. Stack layers; frost sides.
7. Top with additional fudge topping and sliced almonds.
8. Cover and chill until ready to serve; refrigerate leftovers.

E CHRISTMAS HERSHEY-ET COOKIES

Yield: about 24 cookies

15-ounce package sugar cookie mix
1 cup Christmas Hershey-ets
¼ cup red or green sugar crystals

1. Prepare cookie dough according to package directions.
2. Stir in Christmas Hershey-ets.
3. Shape into 1½-inch balls. (Cover dough and chill about 30 minutes if too soft to handle.)
4. Roll in colored sugar crystals.
5. Place 2 inches apart on an ungreased cookie sheet.
6. Bake at 375° for 10 to 12 minutes or until almost set.
7. Leave on cookie sheet about 1 minute.
8. Use spatula to remove from cookie sheet.
9. Place on wire rack to cool.

M PEANUT BUTTER PARTY CONES

Yield: 24 cones

18.25 or 18.5-ounce package yellow cake mix
1½ cups REESE'S Peanut Butter Chips
½ cup milk
24 waffle-type ice cream cones with flat bottoms
2 16-ounce containers any flavor ready-to-spread frosting
Chocolate or colored candy sprinkles

1. Prepare cake batter according to package directions; set aside.
2. Melt REESE'S Peanut Butter Chips with milk in top of double boiler over hot (*not* boiling) water, stirring constantly until blended.
3. Add peanut butter mixture *while warm* to cake batter.
4. Beat on medium speed until blended, about 2 minutes.
5. Fill ice cream cone cups ⅔ to ¾ full with batter.
6. Place upright in regular muffin cups or 2 inches apart on cookie sheet.
7. Bake at 350° for 30 to 35 minutes or until cake tester inserted comes out clean.
8. Cool completely.
9. Frost with ready-to-spread frosting to look like scoops of ice cream.
10. Decorate with chocolate or colored candy sprinkles.

D HOLIDAY COCOA CHEESECAKE

Yield: about 9 servings

    Cocoa Crumb Crust (recipe follows)
½ **cup cold water**
1 **envelope unflavored gelatine**
¼ **cup sugar**
2 **8-ounce packages cream cheese**
½ **cup HERSHEY'S Cocoa**
14-ounce can (1⅓ cups) sweetened
    condensed milk
    **Whipped topping and red or green
    candied cherries**

1. Prepare Cocoa Crumb Crust; set aside to cool.
2. Meanwhile, pour cold water into a small micro-proof bowl.
3. Sprinkle gelatine onto cold water.
4. Let stand 5 minutes to soften gelatine.
5. Microwave on high (full power) for 1 to 1½ minutes or until gelatine is dissolved. (Water will look clear when stirred.)
6. Add sugar and stir until dissolved; set aside.
7. Beat cream cheese on medium speed in a large mixer bowl until softened, about 1 minute.
8. Add HERSHEY'S Cocoa and beat on low speed until moistened.
9. Beat on medium speed until smooth and well blended, about 3 minutes.
10. Blend in condensed milk.
11. Add gelatine-sugar mixture.
12. Beat on medium speed until thoroughly blended, about 3 minutes.
13. Pour into Cocoa Crumb Crust.
14. Cover and chill overnight.
15. Serve with whipped topping and candied cherries; refrigerate leftovers.

Cocoa Crumb Crust

1¼ **cups graham cracker crumbs**
¼ **cup sugar**
2 **tablespoons HERSHEY'S Cocoa**
⅓ **cup butter or margarine**

1. Combine graham cracker crumbs, sugar and HERSHEY'S Cocoa in an 8- or 9-inch square micro-proof dish.
2. Place butter or margarine in the dish with crumb mixture.
3. Microwave on high (full power) for 1 to 1½ minutes or until butter or margarine is melted.
4. Mix with spoon until butter or margarine is blended with other ingredients.
5. Press mixture onto bottom of pan with back of spoon or rubber spatula.

*Holiday Cocoa Cheesecake, this page
Festive Cream-Filled Poundcake, 57
Christmas Hershey-et Cookies, 57*

For Santa
From Paul

Topping It Off

TOPPING IT OFF

Here, and on the pages that follow, are some yummy ideas and recipes for finishing off your favorite desserts and treats...

- For a special treat, sprinkle REESE'S PIECES, HERSHEY'S MINI CHIPS, or HERSHEY'S Milk Chocolate Chips on your homemade ice cream sundaes.
- Decorate Mom's chocolate cream pie with dollops of whipped topping and HERSHEY'S KISSES.
- Scoop your favorite ice cream into any cookie crumb crust (homemade or bought from the grocery store). Top with warm HERSHEY'S Chocolate Fudge Topping, whipped topping, REESE'S Peanut Butter Chips and maraschino cherries for a super sundae pie.
- Slice pound cake and top with scoops of ice cream and sliced fruit. Finish with HERSHEY'S Syrup for an extra special dessert.
- Mix warm HERSHEY'S Chocolate Fudge Topping and HERSHEY'S Syrup (right from the fridge) for a tasty ice cream sauce.
- Chop REESE'S Peanut Butter Chips by hand or in nut chopper (do *not* use food processor or blender). Sprinkle on desserts in place of chopped peanuts.
- Drizzle HERSHEY'S Syrup on frosted cakes to dress them up and make them taste even better.
- Wash and dry fresh strawberries. Dip in melted HERSHEY'S Semi-Sweet Chocolate Chips, MINI CHIPS, or HERSHEY'S SPECIAL DARK Bar. Serve immediately for a good snack.

ALL-IN-ONE SUNDAE TOPPING

Yield: about ¾ cup topping

- **3 1.65-ounce HERSHEY'S MR. GOODBAR Chocolate Bars**
- **3 large marshmallows**
- **2 tablespoons milk**

1. Break HERSHEY'S MR. GOODBAR Chocolate Bars into pieces.
2. Place in top of double boiler with marshmallows and milk.
3. Stir constantly over hot (*not* boiling) water until chocolate and marshmallows are melted and blended. (Do not crush peanuts.)
4. Remove from heat and remove top of double boiler from water.
5. Let stand about 1 minute before serving.
6. Serve warm over your favorite ice cream.

MINI CHIP MARSHMALLOW GLAZE

Yield: about 1 cup

- **⅓ cup sugar**
- **3 tablespoons water**
- **1 cup HERSHEY'S MINI CHIPS**
- **3 tablespoons marshmallow creme**
- **1 to 2 tablespoons hot water**

1. Combine sugar and 3 tablespoons water in a small saucepan.
2. Stir constantly over medium heat *just* until mixture boils.
3. Remove from heat and stir in HERSHEY'S MINI CHIPS until melted and blended.
4. Blend in marshmallow creme.
5. Stir in hot water, 1 teaspoonful at a time, until glaze is desired consistency.
6. Use to glaze cakes, brownies or cookies.

Ⓜ COCOA-CINNAMON TOPPER

Yield: Enough topping for about 12 slices toast

Cocoa-Cinnamon Topping (recipe follows)
Any flavor sliced bread
Butter or margarine

Cocoa-Cinnamon Topping

¼ **cup sugar**
1 **tablespoon HERSHEY'S Cocoa**
2 **teaspoons cinnamon**

1. Thoroughly combine all Topping ingredients in a small bowl.
2. Set aside while preparing toast.

To prepare toast:

1. Place desired amount of bread slices on cookie sheet.
2. Broil 5 inches from heat until golden brown, about 1 minute. (Watch carefully.)
3. Remove from oven and turn slices over so that untoasted side is facing up.
4. Place about 2 teaspoons butter or margarine on each slice of warm toast.
5. Let stand a few minutes to soften butter or margarine.
6. Spread evenly.
7. Sprinkle each slice with about 1 teaspoon Cocoa-Cinnamon Topping.
8. Return to oven and broil about 5 inches from heat until bubbly, about 1 minute. (Watch carefully.)
9. Serve warm.

Ⓔ Tiny Tot's Toast

1. Toast desired amount of bread slices in toaster.
2. Place about 2 teaspoons butter or margarine on each slice of warm toast.
3. Let stand a few minutes to soften butter or margarine.
4. Spread evenly.
5. Sprinkle each slice with about 1 teaspoon Cocoa-Cinnamon Topping.
6. Cut into quarters to serve.

Ⓜ COCOA FROSTING

Yield: about 2 cups

2⅔ **cups unsifted confectioners' sugar**
¾ **cup HERSHEY'S Cocoa**
6 **tablespoons butter or margarine**
⅓ **cup milk**
1 **teaspoon vanilla**

1. Combine confectioners' sugar and HERSHEY'S Cocoa in a small bowl; set aside.
2. Place butter or margarine in a small mixer bowl.
3. Beat until softened.
4. Add ½ *cup* of the confectioners' sugar-cocoa mixture.
5. Beat on low speed until ingredients are moistened.
6. Beat on medium speed until smooth and creamy, about 2 minutes.
7. Gradually add remaining confectioners' sugar-cocoa mixture with milk, beating on low speed.
8. Beat on medium speed to spreading consistency. (An additional tablespoon milk may be needed.)
9. Blend in vanilla.
10. Use to frost your favorite cake or cupcakes.

D ROLO-VER ICE CREAM TOPPING

Yield: about 1½ cups topping

18 ROLO pieces
6 large marshmallows
3 tablespoons milk

1. Place all ingredients in top of double boiler.
2. Stir constantly over hot (*not* boiling) water until ROLO pieces and marshmallows are melted and blended.
3. Remove from heat and remove top of double boiler from water.
4. Let stand about 1 minute before serving.
5. Serve warm over your favorite ice cream.

M CHOCOLATE CARAMEL ICE CREAM SAUCE

Yield: about 1½ cups topping

5.5-ounce can (½ cup) HERSHEY'S Syrup
20 light caramels
3 tablespoons milk
2 tablespoons butter or margarine

1. Place all ingredients in a small micro-proof bowl.
2. Microwave on high (full power) for 2 to 2½ minutes or until caramels are softened.
3. Stir until caramels are melted and blended. (If necessary, microwave on high a few additional seconds to melt caramels.)
4. Serve warm over ice cream.

M BROILED FROSTING CAKE

Yield: about 12 servings

18.25 or 18.5-ounce package white or yellow cake mix
1 cup HERSHEY'S Chocolate Fudge Topping (room temperature)
½ cup flaked coconut
½ cup chopped nuts

1. Prepare cake batter and bake according to package directions for 13 x 9-inch oblong cake; cool about 10 minutes.
2. Meanwhile, combine HERSHEY'S Chocolate Fudge Topping, coconut and chopped nuts in small mixer bowl.
3. Beat on medium speed until blended, about 2 minutes.
4. Spread frosting over warm cake.
5. Broil cake about 5 inches from heat until frosting begins to bubble, about 3 minutes. (Watch carefully.)
6. Serve warm or cool.

E FUDGEY TOPPED FINGERPAINT CAKE

Yield: about 12 servings

18.25 or 18.5-ounce package any flavor cake mix
16-ounce can (1½ cups) HERSHEY'S Chocolate Fudge Topping (room temperature)
Ice cream

1. Prepare cake batter and bake according to package directions for 13 x 9-inch oblong cake.
2. Remove from oven and immediately place heaping tablespoonfuls of HERSHEY'S Chocolate Fudge Topping on top of warm cake.
3. Let stand 15 minutes to soften fudge topping.
4. Gently fingerpaint fudge topping onto cake to frost and make designs.
5. Cool completely.
6. Serve with ice cream; refrigerate leftovers.

Rolo-ver Ice Cream Topping, this page
All-In-One Sundae Topping, 60

Index